BANKRUPTCY FROM A TO Z

THE PATH TO FINANCIAL HOPE AND FREEDOM

BETTY ANNE GRILLO

Publisher: Sunset Dream

BANKRUPTCY FROM A TO Z
The Path to Financial Hope and Freedom

Author's Disclaimer

Legal information is not legal advice. This book is designed to help readers understand their own legal needs and to participate fully in resolving their legal matters. Legal information is not the same as legal advice. Legal advice is the application of the law to the specific circumstances of an individual. Although I go to great lengths to make sure the information in this book is accurate and useful, I highly recommend you consult a lawyer if you want professional assurance that this information, and your interpretation of it, is appropriate to your particular situation. Those seeking specific legal advice or assistance should contact an attorney. This book does not provide investment, tax, or legal advice of any kind. If you need legal advice, legal expertise, or any other type of legal advocacy, you should consult with a licensed attorney in your state.

Printed in the United States of America

Copyright © 2012 by Sunset Dream

First Edition

Copyright © 2012 Betty Anne Grillo
All rights reserved.

ISBN: 0615585698
ISBN 13: 9780615585697

Library of Congress Control Number: 2012930063
Sunset Dream, Kunkletown, PA

To the love of my life, Salvatore.
Your belief in me
allowed the dream within
to be realized.
I am forever grateful.
My life is a paradise with you.

Contents

BASIC TERMS AND CONCEPTS, cont'd

PART TWO
THE PATH TO FINANCIAL FREEDOM
FILING BANKRUPTCY AND BEYOND

ADDITIONAL TERMS AND CONCEPTS

ADDITIONAL TERMS AND CONCEPTS, cont'd

Introduction

I designed this book to educate and empower you to investigate appropriate solutions to your financial problems. This guide is meant to cut through the fear and guilt often associated with filing bankruptcy. It frames the process in the same way you should: as a practical and legal tool used by millions to recover from financial bumps in the road of life.

Utilize it as your guide to gather information, interview attorneys, and seek reliable legal advice. Use it to help you take control of your life beyond the balance in your checkbook. This is a road map crafted by a paralegal who has guided countless others from devastation to a hopeful future.

Whether or not you decide to file bankruptcy, this book will inspire and enlighten you with common-sense tips. It takes a compassionate approach to your current financial situation. Your financial future is in your hands. Make it the best future possible!

Bankruptcy From A To Z

Part One

THE PATH TO FINANCIAL HOPE

BEFORE YOU FILE BANKRUPTCY

One Step at a Time

I know you don't want to read this book. Honestly I wish I hadn't felt the need to write it. You never thought you would be part of a financial horror movie. I understand completely. It seems like a nightmare that just won't end.

We know that sometimes we have to read things we don't want to read and do things we don't want to do. **This book turns your current financial roadblock into a common-sense leap toward the breakthrough.**

You probably don't remember learning your first language as a young child because it was a natural part of growing up. Learning about bankruptcy is different because you never thought you would face this situation. Understanding the language associated with bankruptcy is important at this pivotal time in your life. These pages will educate you about terms specific to bankruptcy, sometimes referred to as legalese. This book translates the bankruptcy knowledge I gained during my career as a paralegal into a common-sense language you can use to your benefit. **Take control of your own financial future.**

You find yourself here after a painful, unexpected personal journey. Your triumph over the pain will be even more personal. Far too many honest, hardworking people like you have made gut-wrenching decisions about bankruptcy. **You are definitely not alone. Bankruptcy can affect anyone.**

I am encouraged that you found the strength to read this book. You confronted your financial problems in an intelligent way, and you will find the solutions to those problems in short order. You have taken the first steps toward reclaiming and restoring your financial freedom.

**You have reached
the point of empowerment.**

Empowerment

I'd like to share a little bit about me. I began working at the age of sixteen. Like most people, I always enjoyed hard work. I was considered a devoted wife, mother, and valued employee; by all indications my life was what I always hoped it would be. I possessed just about everything I needed and most of what I desired.

Without any warning and with no chance to prepare, I found myself widowed at the age of forty-one. A sudden heart attack killed my husband when he was just forty-five years old. My life was changed forever in the blink of an eye. I then suffered through the emotional and psychological strain caused by his death.

At the risk of sounding cold and selfish, I also experienced an unexpected strain: the drastic reduction of household income my family experienced that fateful Monday morning. Unfortunately, the bills didn't decrease by even one penny. In those lonely wee hours of the night, I often thought to myself, "How can I do this alone? Will I have to file bankruptcy?" **One of the most terrifying questions my teenage son asked me right after his father died was, "Mom, will we be OK financially?"**

Imagine that as an experienced paralegal, knowledgeable in bankruptcy matters, I didn't know how to answer his question. Obviously I was not prepared to be the breadwinner of the family. It was evident to me at that moment that this life-changing event was totally beyond my control.

Suddenly I didn't know if I could pay the rent, the bills, or the first installment on the used car we purchased just three weeks before my husband's death. The rising utility bills—barely covered by our two incomes before that tragic day—loomed in front of me.

I faced tough challenges before in my life. Nineteen years prior, my first child suffered a devastating brain injury at birth. That was a life-changing event beyond my control if ever there was one. Finding ways to provide her specialized care taught me many lessons about overcoming challenges. Since then, I've handled many crises. I've risen above them all and bravely pushed through. This crisis, however, was altogether different.

There was a fear and guilt that overcame me like nothing I had ever known. I was raised to meet my obligations, and I took pride in doing so. The awful reality I had to accept now was that I didn't have enough money to go around. Sadly, even my faith was tested. My religious beliefs taught me that God expected me to pay my debts. What was I going to do?

**That dreadful day
changed everything.**

Fortunately the unexpected challenges in my life helped me develop empathy and compassion for the clients who crossed my path in the years that followed. While working in a high-volume law firm for eighteen years, I assisted countless numbers of clients with their bankruptcy cases. Every day I worked diligently to help turn the agony they suffered into optimism, their fears into understanding. It was never "just a job" for me. Just as I asked those clients on many occasions, I recommend that you tuck the following phrase into the back of your mind until you believe it in your heart:

Out of the worst that could happen comes the best that can be.

I am not an attorney, and you must know these very important facts:

**I cannot give you legal advice.
I cannot represent you in court.**

The law permits only licensed attorneys to provide these essential services. An attorney has a law degree and has passed the bar exam, setting him or her apart from friends and family. The best attorneys have acquired vast experience in bankruptcy law by handling intricate cases.

Anyone who advises you to file bankruptcy, other than an
attorney, violates the law
by practicing without a license.

If filing bankruptcy could be the solution to your financial problems, I strongly urge you to hire an effective attorney to explore your options.

This is one crisis you should not handle without the
advice of counsel.

I hope you now understand my motivation more clearly. Kindly permit me to share some insight as you search for the attorney who best suits your circumstances. We can then walk together on the journey that lies ahead.

Educate yourself by reading at least the first section of this book prior to filing bankruptcy, and become familiar with the basic terms and concepts listed here. Allow me to demonstrate what this book can do for you. I am confident it will help you navigate the road map for your journey toward a bright financial future.

You'll find explanations for many of the legal terms you will encounter concerning finances and bankruptcy. You should become familiar with the terms and concepts before you meet with an attorney. This will help you select the best attorney for the circumstances and understand the legal advice you receive. You will be able to work with that attorney from day one to determine the right course, which will empower you to decide whether bankruptcy is the solution for your situation.

The most comprehensive parts of this book are the two alphabetical lists of terms and concepts used throughout the bankruptcy process. These will soon become the foundation of an easily understood, common-sense language. Your attorney will provide more details about each term that applies to your situation.

The first list includes the basic terms and concepts you should learn before you decide to file bankruptcy. This list will help you comprehend the legal advice you receive. The second list contains more advanced terms and the guidance you will need after you decide to file bankruptcy. This user-friendly book provides tools to help you embark on the best financial path available at this time in your life.

My focus on the personal journey experienced by each individual inspired me to write this book. That focus and inspiration continues today. My interactions with countless clients convinced me of my destiny to serve as a guide for many others I would never personally meet, just like you.

The attorney considers your complete financial history, so be prepared to provide as much information as possible. Know the legal terms the attorney will use before you go into that first meeting. It will give you an advantage over those who don't do their homework ahead of time. **Be prepared prior to the initial consultation. Do not make decisions that could dramatically affect your life without first understanding the basic language.**

As a paralegal, I act as the bridge between the client and the attorney in order to explain and simplify the process. Most importantly this book explains in simple terms the legalese you will encounter when you meet with and then hire an attorney.

Prepare yourself, and seek detailed answers from a qualified attorney as soon as you can. You will receive sound legal advice pertinent to your situation. This book provides the information needed to become your own best advocate throughout this very serious undertaking.

Preparation is the key to your success.

Overcome Your Fears

FEARS: We all have them. Some fears are rooted in facts, but most are based on fears of the unknown. Thinking about filing bankruptcy does not make you more fearful than the next person, but there are specific fears that relate directly to bankruptcy.

Particular fears that clients shared with me pertained to the attorney and staff handling their case. Here are some of the most common fears concerning bankruptcy:

1. Will the attorney think I'm stupid?
2. Will these people judge me because I didn't pay my bills?
3. Do they talk about me with their family and friends?
4. Will the attorney talk down to me because he or she went to law school?
5. Should I ask a question or try to figure it out on my own so I don't look bad?
6. Will I be treated like a number instead of an individual?
7. Have I hired a good attorney?
8. Will the attorney and staff treat me with respect?
9. Will my attorney meet all of the deadlines in my case?
10. Is there another way to solve my money problems without filing bankruptcy?
11. Why does it cost so much to file bankruptcy?
12. Can I trust the attorney to look out for me?
13. Will the attorney return my phone calls?
14. Will I understand what the attorney tells me?

Some of these questions may have already crossed your mind. Perhaps there are others you hadn't thought to ask yet. In the following pages, you will find the information needed to make your fears fade away and develop the courage to seek professional advice. Over time you will feel less afraid and become more powerful.

You can move beyond the desperation of your current situation toward the hopeful path of financial prosperity.

The Attorney Works For You

There are two things to remember when you first interview an attorney:

> You are the boss, and
> your future is at stake.

You choose an attorney to provide you with professional services as you would a doctor or plumber. Most of the information you encounter will be new to you. I encourage you to learn the terms explained in this book so you can monitor your legal situation effectively.

You are not too old to learn, but you are important enough to believe in a better future. **This book was written to restore hope—your financial hope.**

In the section, "The Path to Financial Hope: Basic Legal Terms and Concepts," you will find an alphabetical list of some of the most common bankruptcy terms. You will confront these terms now that your journey to financial hope has begun. **Ask your attorney how these legal terms relate to your financial situation. Now let's continue the journey toward hope together.**

> There is no better place to start
> than with the letter A.

THE PATH TO FINANCIAL HOPE
Basic Terms And Concepts

A

ADVICE Everyone you discuss your situation with will try to give you advice. Step away from your brother-in-law, your neighbor, your aunt, or anyone else who shares his or her "legal knowledge" of bankruptcy with you. **Their advice is not legal advice. Smile politely, and then walk away.** Their perspectives merely reflect personal opinions of your financial situation. Such advice is worthless and could prove harmful if you follow it.

As mentioned earlier I am a paralegal, not an attorney. I cannot provide legal advice or represent you in court. I can, however, show you where to find answers and legal advice. Bypass your friends, your family, and the neighborhood busybody. **Contact the only person who can legally, professionally, and intelligently advise you: a competent attorney.**

ASSETS The court will evaluate your assets during the bankruptcy process. These assets include the combined value of all real estate and personal property you own when you file your case.

ATTORNEY SELECTION If you haven't received a lawyer referral from someone you trust, you can call your local bar association. This group maintains a list of attorneys in a particular county that includes their areas of practice. Some bar associations will even contact an attorney's office to make an appointment for you, usually for a small fee. Using this resource assures that you only meet attorneys who are in good standing with the legal community.

You should interview at least two attorneys before making a final choice. **The cheapest attorney may not necessarily be the best choice.** The least expensive attorney might be inexperienced and could potentially provide the lowest level of service. **Choose carefully.**

<u>AUTOMATIC STAY</u> This term describes the hold put on most legal actions against you when you officially file a bankruptcy case. Perhaps you face a hearing because of a lawsuit filed in the local magistrate or county court; that lawsuit might have prompted you to consider bankruptcy.

A bankruptcy case is filed in federal court. Once you file, the parties to any pending lawsuits against you in other courts must request permission from the bankruptcy court to continue pursuing their case.

<u>AUTOMOBILES</u> Any automobiles you own are considered part of your assets. You must tell the attorney about all vehicles titled in your name. This includes any vehicles for which you have co-signed, even if someone else makes the payments. **A vehicle is generally considered one of your assets if you signed on the loan or your name appears on the title.**

Even if you own a vehicle outright, you must provide the year, make, model, and private party value for that car. You must indicate whether you own it individually or jointly, and provide the name, address, and relationship of anyone else listed on the title.

B

BANK ACCOUNTS Anyone reading this book most likely has a bank account in his or her name. In addition to your personal accounts, these accounts include checking and savings accounts for children, business operating accounts, and even those accounts containing a few dollars put away for the holidays. Disclose all bank accounts to your attorney so the portion of the assets protected from your creditors by law can be determined.

Most people do not have to give up the funds in these accounts; much of their personal property is exempt and will not be used to pay creditors.

BANK STATEMENTS Your bank statements show the transactions made in your accounts—including business accounts and accounts you hold jointly with other parties—each month. **All bank statements for the six-month period prior to filing your case must be provided to your attorney.**

BILL COLLECTORS In some cases bill collectors work for the original creditors to collect your outstanding balance. It's also possible that a company purchased your account from the original creditor at a reduced price, happy to collect just pennies on the dollar since they control thousands of accounts. These companies can make a lot of money on delinquent accounts. An attorney's office may also be in the business of collecting overdue bills.

Bill collectors will continue to call you, send nasty letters, and make your life miserable until you either pay what you owe, negotiate a settlement, or file bankruptcy.

Meet with an attorney before you send any more money to a bill collector. **Ask the attorney what to do about future payments to creditors. It might be better to save the money and put it toward attorney fees so you can file bankruptcy. Seek the advice of a competent attorney immediately.** If you decide to file bankruptcy, the debts could be discharged in the process. Don't waste your hard-earned money unnecessarily.

BILLS Your outstanding bills can include: the deficiency balance on a repossessed car, a mortgage on real estate, past-due utility bills, medical expenses, and many other categories of debt. Due to high interest rates, penalties, and hidden fees, you might never expect to completely pay off these balances. **If you find it necessary to file bankruptcy, be certain to include all debts you owe at the time of filing.**

BUDGET Preparing a budget you can control easily and realistically will become part of your life when you file bankruptcy. When completing the worksheets for your attorney, you must list all income (gross and net), and then compare that income to your ongoing monthly expenses. This process helps you create a monthly budget.

Many people told me that prior to filing bankruptcy, they had never established a household budget. That may have contributed to their out-of-control spending. Pay particular attention to the necessity of your purchases. What has been said for so many years still rings true: if you take care of the pennies, the dollars will take care of themselves.

C

CHAPTER 7 BANKRUPTCY Most people considering bankruptcy hope to qualify for Chapter 7. The qualifying process begins with passing the Means Test (your gross income must be below the maximum set by the office of the US Trustee). Under Chapter 7 bankruptcy, you usually have protection from any creditors who attempt to collect on unsecured debts.

CHAPTER 7 TRUSTEE The court assigns a trustee to each bankruptcy case. **The trustee represents neither the debtor(s) nor the creditor(s) in a case.** It is the duty of the trustee to verify to the court that a case conforms to the various aspects of bankruptcy law in any particular financial situation.

The trustee also determines if the debtor provided truthful information concerning income and assets. Your attorney must have a good working relationship with the trustee. Provide any information requested by the trustee—such as bank statements and tax returns—to your attorney as soon as possible. **The Chapter 7 trustee verifies your qualification as a Chapter 7 debtor; he or she also determines whether any assets should be sold to pay your debts.**

CHAPTER 13 BANKRUPTCY A debtor may have to file a Chapter 13 bankruptcy case if his or her gross income is above the Means Test amount allowed for his or her household size, even after subtracting any allowable expenses. Chapter 13 might also be appropriate if a debtor wants to keep his or her house, but needs three to five years to catch up on past-due mortgage payments.

A debtor's assets might be valued higher than the exemptions allowed by law. In order to keep those assets, a Chapter 13 case could be filed. If someone wants to file bankruptcy within eight years of filing a prior Chapter 7 case, it may be necessary for him or her to file Chapter 13 instead.

Ask an attorney for advice about how the situations listed above could affect your bankruptcy case.

CHILD SUPPORT PAYMENTS Court-ordered child support payments are considered in the Means Test. **Provide copies of your most recent child support Order(s) to the attorney at the initial consultation.** The court requires copies of those Orders, and the documents will be reviewed by the trustee in all cases.

CHILDREN **Bankruptcy affects children in ways you might not notice.** Be honest with your children, and determine what information will be easily understood by them. Always listen to the concerns of your child. **Once you eliminate financial stress, life improves for everyone.**

CIVIL LITIGATION This refers to being sued over something other than a criminal matter. Many people sued by banks or credit card companies find it necessary to file bankruptcy. Others face mortgage foreclosure and other types of civil actions. **Inform your attorney of any and all lawsuits immediately.**

CO-DEBTOR (pronounced "co-detter") This person is jointly obligated to pay back a debt. If you and your spouse have co-signed a loan or credit card, you are co-debtors. **All co-debtors can be pursued individually by creditors.** It is important to share information about co-debtors with your attorney so he or she can determine whether you should file jointly or as an individual. This determination depends on who actually owes the debts.

Sometimes a co-debtor is someone who co-signs for another party, as when a parent co-signs for his or her adult child. A co-debtor is responsible for the entire debt if the person he or she co-signed for does not repay the loan. **Creditors will pursue anyone they can in order to recover money owed to them.**

COLLATERAL This is the property a creditor can take from you if you do not pay a debt according to the terms of your agreement. **Bring copies of all available loan documents to your initial consultation.**

COLLECTION AGENCY (*See BILL COLLECTORS*)

COMMUNICATION One of the most important factors in choosing an attorney is your ability to communicate well with that attorney and his or her staff.

A reliable attorney wants to keep the lines of communication between you and his or her office open and straightforward. If you feel that communication is a problem, discuss the matter directly with the attorney or an office manager. Do not allow a lack of communication to worsen before bringing it to someone's attention.

You will receive better communication from an attorney if you communicate well yourself. Treat the attorney and his or her staff with respect. They are not the enemy. They work along with you to solve your financial and legal problems.

CONSUMER LIABILITY REPORT This is another name for your credit report. When your attorney prepares the bankruptcy paperwork, he or she will acquire your consumer liability report. You must sign an authorization form to grant the attorney permission to obtain that report. There is a charge for the report, which you must pay. A joint (debtor and spouse) credit report will cost more than one obtained for an individual.

Before hiring an attorney, find out what services are covered by his or her fee and what additional costs you will have to pay. A reputable attorney will not have any hidden costs.

CREDIT REPORT (*See CONSUMER LIABILITY REPORT*).

CREDIT COUNSELING REQUIREMENT A requirement was added to the bankruptcy filing process in 2005 that addresses the debtor's budget prior to filing. With few exceptions, the credit counseling requirement must be completed with a court-approved provider at least twenty-four hours prior to filing bankruptcy. This provision was instituted to curtail the practice of filing bankruptcy at the last minute for the sole purpose of putting a Sheriff's Sale on hold in foreclosure cases. Though relatively few people used this tactic, the credit counseling requirement now affects nearly everyone who files bankruptcy.

CREDITOR A creditor is anyone you owe money to at the time of filing bankruptcy. You cannot omit any creditors from your bankruptcy case; all creditors of the same class (secured, priority, or unsecured) must be treated equally.

You cannot list a Visa card, for example, but choose to omit a department store card so you can continue using it. *All* unsecured, secured, and priority creditors must be listed on your paperwork.

CURRENT MONTHLY INCOME When the bankruptcy laws changed in 2005, the term *Current Monthly Income* (CMI) came into being. CMI is determined by adding all gross income you (the debtor and joint debtor, if applicable) received for the six-month period prior to filing bankruptcy. That figure is doubled to determine annual income and then divided by twelve to determine your monthly income. Your attorney will explain the importance of the CMI calculation in your case.

D

DEBT RELIEF AGENCY Since bankruptcy law allows debtors to receive relief from their debts, the law requires offices whose attorneys advise and subsequently file bankruptcies to be referred to as *Debt Relief Agencies*. You might notice this term on the letterhead of your attorney's office. **Attorneys who practice bankruptcy law must inform the public that they provide this service.**

DEBTOR (pronounced "detter") A debtor is anyone who owes money to another party. If you are the person filing bankruptcy, you are referred to as the debtor in the case. Your spouse is identified as the co-debtor if it is a joint filing.

Some of the terms you hear your attorney and others use might be foreign to you. **Understanding the terms and how to pronounce them will give you added confidence and increased control over the situation.**

DISCHARGE You will receive a discharge of your debts after successfully completing the full process in either Chapter 7 or 13 bankruptcy. This means that creditors can no longer collect on your debts unless the bankruptcy court determines a specific debt to be non-dischargeable. **Ask your attorney if any of your debts might be considered non-dischargeable by the court.**

DISMISSAL Sometimes a bankruptcy case is dismissed by the court. **If this happens the debtor no longer has protection under bankruptcy law, and his or her case is closed.** A debtor can also request a voluntary dismissal of their bankruptcy. Discuss this section of the law in detail with your attorney so you fully understand how a dismissal action would affect your case.

DISPOSABLE INCOME When you file a bankruptcy case, your attorney provides paperwork to the court that lists your income and expenses. The federal government sets guidelines for these amounts by using IRS standards for your geographical area.

Any income that remains after paying all allowable expenses is referred to as disposable income. This amount is especially important in Chapter 13 bankruptcy because it is one factor used to determine how much will be paid into a Chapter 13 Debtor's Plan.

DOCTOR BILLS **Outstanding doctor bills and medical expenses can be included in your bankruptcy filing. Even veterinary bills can be listed.** These bills can skyrocket to an amount that you could never repay. The court generally treats these bills like other unsecured debts, such as credit cards and personal loans.

DOCUMENTS You will review and sign many documents over the course of a bankruptcy case. **I can't stress strongly enough that you must first review—and understand—everything you sign.** It has always been my practice to review documents page by page with clients. I would point out terms that might be unfamiliar to them so that I knew they understood what they were signing. Insist that your attorney carefully reviews all documents with you. **Signing a document that is filed with the court makes you personally responsible for its contents.** The court doesn't want to hear that you didn't understand the document but signed it anyway.

From the Voluntary Petition, which is the first document filed in your case, to a Reaffirmation Agreement or Chapter 13 Debtor's Plan, each document filed with the court states that you have provided true and correct information and that you will perform a certain duty or action. Be well-informed before signing any document.

Your financial future depends on it.

E

EDUCATION LOANS Education loans are also called student loans. Even though these debts are usually owed to the government, they are listed on the unsecured creditors section of the bankruptcy paperwork (Schedule F).

Sometimes an education loan is owed to a private lender. It is possible that this type of loan can be discharged by the court. **Your attorney will know if your education loan can be discharged.**

ELIGIBILITY **Many people fear their bankruptcy case will not be approved by the court. This is not something to be concerned about. I** don't know where these fears began, but countless people are afraid that it will happen to them.

A debtor may file a Chapter 13 case instead of Chapter 7 in order to pay back some of his or her creditors. He or she might file Chapter 7 and then convert to a Chapter 13 bankruptcy later to save property that might be at risk. Your attorney will know what is best in your situation.

EMBARRASSMENT This emotion has been felt by so many clients that I could sense their pain as they sat across the desk from me. **I convinced them that filing bankruptcy should be considered nothing more than a financial matter.** Many people walked into my office in tears but left feeling that some of the weight had been lifted from their shoulders.

They learned that bankruptcy is a financial tool permitted by law. That reality helped lift the weight of embarrassment from them.

EMPLOYER People are afraid their employers and co-workers will find out about their bankruptcy filing. Many employers and even some of your co-workers may have filed bankruptcy. They won't treat you badly even if they find out.

Most importantly the bankruptcy court does not contact your employer or send notices to your place of work. Your employer and co-workers would not normally find out about your bankruptcy case unless you told them or listed them as a creditor.

EXEMPT PROPERTY Exempt property is property in your possession that cannot be sold by the trustee to pay balances you owe to creditors. Some examples of exempt property include: the positive equity in your home and/or vehicle, household goods, jewelry, cash on hand, money deposited in bank accounts, retirement accounts, firearms, IRAs, security deposits, clothing, life insurance policies, pensions, and tools of the trade. **These exemptions cannot exceed the guidelines set by the US Trustee.**

EXEMPTIONS You are entitled to specific exemptions concerning your property in a bankruptcy case. Most people are afraid they will have to automatically turn their property over to the bankruptcy court, and that they may lose their home, cars, or other property. **Fortunately the court recognizes that you need certain property in order to live and support your family.**

These exemption amounts vary from state to state and district to district. Districts are the specific regions covered by each geographical area of the bankruptcy court and the respective trustees. **Your attorney can answer specific questions about your exemptions.**

EXPECTATIONS The debtor's expectations in a bankruptcy case sometimes affect the journey he or she must endure. **Filing bankruptcy is a significant action on your part. Your expectations should be guided by facts, not by emotions.** What others have experienced in their bankruptcy cases has nothing to do with your situation. Trust your attorney to guide you through this very individual process.

A bankruptcy is usually more time-consuming than expected. The attorney has to meet many deadlines in each case. Every situation is unique. **Be realistic** when discussing your financial situation with your attorney. Listen receptively to even the most difficult advice.

Keep looking ahead to life after bankruptcy. It's comparable to swallowing unpleasant medicine now so you'll feel better later. When you face the situation head on, follow the legal advice you receive, and **work with your attorney to achieve the best outcome**, you can expect your life to change.

EXPENSES Just as all gross income you receive will be taken into account on your bankruptcy paperwork, all of your expenses will also be listed. The Schedule J section of your bankruptcy paperwork lists all monthly expenses you will continue to pay after you file.

The attorney will advise you of the eligibility of any expenses that are currently in your budget. **Provide the attorney with a detailed list of all items you consider expenses.** If you don't list them, you won't be permitted to claim them.

F

FALSE STATEMENTS Bankruptcy cases are governed by federal law and filed in the federal court system. Any documents you provide or statements you make that are knowingly false will be questioned by the trustee. Unless you want to face severe consequences, tell the truth during the bankruptcy process. Trustees in each district see hundreds if not thousands of cases every year. They are trained to spot conflicting statements. A trustee will determine whether you made dishonest statements on your paperwork.

FAMILY Financial problems affect your family members significantly. Let's face it: no one is happy if there isn't enough money to go around. I know you're being pulled in different directions to provide what each person in your household needs or wants. It's time to be honest with your spouse, your children, and anyone else in your household who is affected by the budget you must now follow. It is time to tighten your financial belt. Stop indulging in unnecessary purchases. Looking ahead to a brighter future will make the sacrifices worthwhile.

FEDERAL BANKRUPTCY LAW Federal bankruptcy laws have been in effect since the 1800s. There have been revisions, repeals, and total upheavals in the laws along the way. The most recent change took place in October, 2005.

The 2005 laws enacted by Congress attempt to correct blatant abuses of bankruptcy law. Unfortunately the few people who filed fraudulent or questionable bankruptcies under the old laws made the process much more difficult for anyone filing after October, 2005.

Credit card companies also gained additional collection tools. The law now allows some of their claims to be paid. Prior to October, 2005, very little money was paid back to unsecured creditors if someone filed bankruptcy.

You can argue the good and bad points of the 2005 law for hours, but the bottom line is that this is now the law you must follow to file bankruptcy.

FEE DISCLOSURE Your attorney must file a Fee Disclosure with the bankruptcy court. **There are limits on how much your attorney can be paid to handle your case without requesting court permission to receive more.** You must review, understand, and sign the Fee Disclosure before it is filed with the court. An attorney's application for higher fees must be approved by the court.

FINANCIAL DECISIONS Your financial decisions up to this point have **been both good and bad. You are no different from anyone else.** Now you should involve a professional trained to advise you about your current financial decisions. Filing bankruptcy may turn out to be the best decision for you. **Do not make this decision on the advice of a friend or family member.** Reach out to hire the attorney who has the legal knowledge and experience to guide you through the challenges you face at this time in your life.

FINANCIAL MANAGEMENT COURSE After you file a Chapter 7 or Chapter 13 case, you must complete a Financial Management Course through a court-approved agency. **This course fulfills the second portion of the educational requirement when you file bankruptcy.** The first requirement is the Credit Counseling Course you take prior to filing.

Your attorney will provide information about the agency to use for these courses. The financial management course can be completed online or over the phone. **If you do not complete this course within the time period mandated by law, you will not receive a discharge in your bankruptcy.**

FORECLOSURE If you currently have a mortgage on your home, there is a good chance you can't make your payments on time. You might be making your mortgage payments as agreed, but your home is worth significantly less than it was just a few years ago. Sadly you may be suffering both of these circumstances. **In these difficult economic times, you are not alone if you face foreclosure.**

If you aren't making your monthly payments as agreed, it is only a matter of time before the mortgage company files a foreclosure action. A foreclosure lawsuit is filed in the county or local court where the property is located. **Filing bankruptcy can put foreclosure actions on hold.** Once you've provided all necessary information, and with your complete cooperation, a qualified, motivated attorney can complete the filing process in just a few days.

There is a court-ordered obligation to complete the Credit Counseling Course at least twenty-four hours before filing bankruptcy. Providing your attorney with all requested information is of the utmost importance and necessary for preparing your case. **Act promptly so your attorney has enough time to delay any foreclosure action.**

FRIENDS We know that our friends generally mean well. Most everyone in this day and age knows someone who has filed bankruptcy. I want to stress again that your friends and family are not attorneys (unless they have law degrees and have passed the bar exam). Their bankruptcy experiences—or those of their aunts, uncles, brothers, or mothers—do not pertain to you. **Obtain your legal advice directly from an attorney.**

G

GOALS I hope that one of your goals is to enjoy a better financial future. If your attorney advises bankruptcy, set new goals that include living within your means and being realistic about your monthly budget. Put money aside that will only be used as a rainy-day fund after filing your bankruptcy case.

GROSS INCOME Your gross income is the total of what you earn before any expenses are subtracted, such as payroll taxes, health insurance premiums, or union dues. It also includes any overtime or bonuses you receive. Your attorney will request pay stubs that clearly show your gross income and all deductions for the six-month period prior to filing.

If you are self-employed, your gross income is the total amount you receive from customers or product sales before subtracting the costs of doing business. The court uses your gross income figure to complete the Means Test. This helps determine which chapter of bankruptcy you will file.

H

HAPPINESS You know as well as I do that your happiness is often linked to your financial situation. **Money can't buy happiness, but a lack of money sure does zap the joy from your day.** At this time in your life, it may seem like you will never be happy again.

You just might feel happier when you complete a bankruptcy case than you did prior to filing it. **Relieving the stress in your life will make room for happiness to grow.**

HOME Your home is a refuge, perhaps even a symbol of having achieved a certain level of success in your life. You are probably afraid you could lose your home. The attorney you choose needs to understand that fear.

Ask your attorney the tough, emotional questions that pertain to your house, and then follow the advice he or she gives you. This advice will not be based on an emotional attachment to the building in which you live; it will be an impartial view of your current financial situation. **Listen to the answers the attorney provides to those tough questions about your home. This sensitive issue requires good communication between you and the attorney.**

HOUSEHOLD GOODS Household goods are considered personal property. They include: furniture, televisions, appliances, clothing, and anything else you might find in the household goods section of a store. **Even if you received an item as a gift, you must include it on the bankruptcy paperwork.**

There are generous exemptions for personal property because the bankruptcy court does not want you to end up on the streets. **You are permitted to keep what the court determines is necessary to rebuild your life.**

<u>HOUSEHOLD SIZE</u> Household size is determined by the number of adults living with you who receive support from you and all dependents you claim on your tax return. **Household size is a factor used to establish the outcome of the Means Test.** In order to avoid problems later, list only individuals allowed by law for this important requirement.

I

IMPORTANT INFORMATION NOTICE A Notice of Important Information About Bankruptcy Assistance Services must be supplied to you by the attorney at the first consultation. Anyone who discusses bankruptcy with an attorney must sign an authorization allowing the attorney to provide legal advice concerning bankruptcy. This legal requirement makes it improper for an attorney to give bankruptcy advice over the phone.

INCOME EXCLUSIONS Some types of income are excluded from the Means Test. They can include social security and social security- disability income. Other income exclusions include payments received by victims of crime or terrorism, or the income of a non-filing spouse who is legally separated from you.

INDIVIDUAL RETIREMENT ACCOUNTS Individual Retirement Accounts (IRAs) and tax-qualified retirement funds may either be exempt under federal bankruptcy law or applicable state law. You must check with your attorney to determine whether a particular IRA is considered exempt.

INTERVIEWING AN ATTORNEY Schedule interviews with at least two different attorneys before hiring one to handle your bankruptcy. Make the choice that is right for you. There are some very important factors to consider before making that choice.

The ability to work well with an attorney depends on your comfort level with his or her individual style. Some attorneys are laid back and relaxed;

others are high-energy, ambitious individuals who never seem to take a breath. The support staff normally reflects the style of the attorney for whom they work. It is important that you get along with the attorney so the lines of communication remain open and honest. You must confirm the staff is professional and knowledgeable in their approach to bankruptcy.

These are the important factors that go into making your hiring decision. If you are not sure about any of these issues after the first visit with an attorney, request a second consultation. You can use that time to clarify the advice you previously received, and ask any additional questions.

A reputable attorney will allow you the opportunity for this additional meeting so you can be confident in your decision to use his or her services.

J

JOINT FILING You are permitted to file a joint bankruptcy case with your spouse. You can file jointly even if you were not married at the time debts were incurred. Each debt will be listed separately, and the bankruptcy document will note which party owes the debt. Many couples have joint and individual debts. These debts can be listed in the same bankruptcy case.

Even if you are married, it doesn't mean you have to file jointly. Your spouse does not have to agree to file bankruptcy with you. This sometimes comes into play when couples are separated or going through a divorce. Either spouse can file an individual bankruptcy if it is in their best interest to do so. The attorney will give you advice that pertains to your particular situation.

JUDGE A judge will be assigned to your case when it is filed. Each judge handles a particular district within the bankruptcy court, depending on geographical location.

The attorney you hire to represent you must be aware of the judge's past rulings in situations relevant to your case. Knowing the judge and his or her prior rulings could come into play concerning property and other issues. It may be smart to continue searching for an attorney if the ones you meet don't file a large number of bankruptcies. It is easier for an attorney to determine the outcome of your case if he or she has represented several clients in situations similar to yours.

Judges are usually very consistent in their rulings. It is part of an attorney's job to know how these rulings could relate to your case. Do your homework by researching bankruptcy before you get in over your head. Be sure the attorney you hire has done the same.

K

KEEP YOUR STRESS LEVEL LOW You will need less stress in your life so you can move forward when the bankruptcy process is over. I can't emphasize enough that knowing the bankruptcy process prior to filing will greatly diminish stress. You will begin to feel like you are in control of your life again.

The most positive side of bankruptcy is that less of your energy will be spent on stress, and more of your energy will be focused on improving your life. You can do this. Your financial future depends on it.

Taking the initiative to read this book will prove very beneficial to you. The information provided here will guide you on your way and ease your worries over time.

KNOWLEDGE You have heard countless times that knowledge is a major key to success. A bankruptcy case could become the most important focus of your current attention. The more knowledgeable you become about credit terms and financial matters, the more successful you will be after your case closes.

You know what they say—you are never too old to learn. Take advantage of the knowledgeable people around you, and learn all you can from them. The important lessons you learn now will prevent you from undergoing another bankruptcy in the future.

I can't stress enough that your attorney should speak with you in a way that makes you feel comfortable and hopeful. Some attorneys talk down to their clients and others who don't have the same level of legal knowledge they possess. The way an attorney treats his or her staff sometimes indicates how the attorney will act toward clients.

If you sense this attitude from an attorney you meet with, it is probably best to keep looking, no matter how good his or her legal reputation may be. **Bankruptcy is a life-changing process. You deserve to be treated with respect and dignity. Don't settle for anything less from your attorney.**

L

LANDLORD MATTERS Perhaps you rented an apartment or house and now find it impossible to pay the rent. Maybe you lost your spouse, your job, or even your good health, and now you can't afford to live at the rented property. A certain provision of the bankruptcy law may affect you.

If your landlord obtained an Order of Eviction from the court, the Automatic Stay in effect in a new bankruptcy case may not prevent you from being evicted. **When there is a dispute concerning money owed to a landlord, the person filing bankruptcy may have to deposit funds with the court when they file until things are sorted out.** A good attorney will provide legal advice concerning how this portion of the law could affect you.

LAWSUITS After the new bankruptcy law was enacted in 2005, the number of civil lawsuits rose dramatically. **Unsecured creditors now often times receive funds through the bankruptcy court from a person who has filed bankruptcy.** Credit card companies push cases through the county court systems, and their customers may find it necessary to file bankruptcy. **If you receive a notice from any court that you have been sued, meet with an attorney immediately.**

LEGAL ADVICE As emphasized in previous pages, it is extremely important that you interview at least two attorneys prior to choosing one to work for you. **Only an attorney can legally represent you in bankruptcy court. Some people attempt to file on their own, but then find it necessary to hire an**

attorney anyway. Attorneys play an important role by negotiating with the court and creditors in ways that debtors are not prepared to handle.

You would not play doctor with your medical concerns, and you shouldn't play attorney with your legal matters. Allow trained professionals to do the work for you.

<u>LIABILITIES</u> Bills and outstanding balances you owe to others are considered liabilities. If you have a house, your mortgage debt is the liability. Car loans and credit card debts are also liabilities. **The liabilities you owe when you file bankruptcy will be listed on the paperwork.**

<u>LIEN</u> A lien is represented by a document filed with the court. The lien places a security interest in the property that secures the debt you owe to a creditor. **When a lien has been placed on your property, you are not free to sell it without first paying off or otherwise satisfying the lien.**

Your attorney must be informed of any lawsuits and liens. Old or new, these legal issues will affect your ability to maintain control of your property. An attorney will handle these matters properly in your bankruptcy case.

<u>LIEN HOLDER</u> **A lien holder is the party you owe money to who can take property back if you do not pay the full balance.** This could be your mortgage company or the bank that holds your car loan. The name of the lien holder is listed on the mortgage paperwork or car title.

Lien holders also include credit card companies who have won a judgment against you in court and filed a lien against your property. A creditor who filed a lien with the court prevents you from disposing of or selling your property without first paying off the lien. **The bankruptcy court addresses the rights of any creditor who holds a lien against your property.** Ask your attorney how this affects you.

M

MANDATORY DEDUCTIONS These deductions can include—among other things—union dues, spousal or child support obligations, and payments for uniform processing fees. You can find them on your pay stubs.

Provide detailed descriptions of your mandatory deductions so the allowable expenses are included by the attorney and staff.

MARITAL PROBLEMS The stress caused by financial problems often weakens the family structure. **Talk openly and honestly with your spouse to see if solving money problems might also solve your marital problems.**

MEANS TEST The Means Test has been a mandatory provision of bankruptcy law since 2005. The test is used to calculate a debtor's *current monthly income* (CMI). **The simple way to explain the Means Test is that if you have the *means* to do so, you are required by the court to pay back your creditors.**

Even if you qualify as a Chapter 7 debtor, you can decide to file a Chapter 13 bankruptcy. It may be possible to save your home or other property this way. Chapter 13 could be beneficial if you are significantly past due on your mortgage payments.

MEDIAN INCOME Median income figures are determined by the IRS for each area of the country. **These figures are used by the court to set the maximum income you can make and still qualify as a Chapter 7 debtor.** If you don't qualify initially for Chapter 7, your attorney will perform a detailed Means Test. This will determine if your itemized expenses reduce your median income enough to show that you do not have the means to repay your creditors.

You can find the most recent median income figures at http://www.justice. gov/ust. Click on the link for median income, and find your state on the tables listed there.

<u>MONTHLY INCOME</u> Your monthly income is a major factor in determining whether you file a Chapter 7 or Chapter 13. **Your attorney will need all pay stubs, all social security statements, and any other statements that show the income you and other members of your household received for the previous six months.** If you are self-employed, you must provide the attorney with gross income figures for each of the six months prior to filing bankruptcy.

After determining your monthly income, the attorney will assess whether you qualify for Chapter 7 bankruptcy. Detailed, complete income information is necessary for your attorney to properly advise you. **Give the attorney all the tools he or she needs to provide you with sound legal advice.** You can then make an informed decision about filing bankruptcy. The attorney will advise how Chapter 7 and Chapter 13 relate to your particular financial situation.

N

NET INCOME Net income is determined by first adding all income sources, then subtracting all taxes and allowable deductions. Your attorney will advise you regarding investments and other sources of income.

The court only allows certain expenses to be deducted from your gross income for the purpose of determining net income. The attorney will know which expenses are allowed by law.

NEW OUTLOOK I sincerely hope you develop a new outlook on your financial future while going through the bankruptcy process. The Financial Management Course will instruct you about finances and living within a budget. Completing the task will feel like a chore, but you will acquire knowledge and discipline during the process.

You owe it to yourself to take the important steps now to ensure your future is better than your past.

NON-FILING SPOUSE A non-filing spouse is a person married to the debtor in a bankruptcy case who has not joined in filing bankruptcy. Sometimes only one spouse has debts and/or assets in his or her name. That affects whether a person files individually even though he or she is married. **Certain states allow protections for marital property if only one spouse files bankruptcy.** Property may be protected if only one spouse files depending on the laws of a particular state.

Ask your attorney if these provisions could apply to you. **Good legal advice determines if there is a benefit to only one spouse filing a bankruptcy case.**

O

OPEN COMMUNICATION Just as in all other relationships in your life, the one between you and your attorney requires open and honest communication. Since you are the party most affected by bankruptcy—and the one who knows the least about the process—you should be the one asking the most questions.

If there is poor communication between you, your attorney, and his or her staff, you are guaranteed to be upset with the legal representation you receive. Your financial future depends on an excellent result from your bankruptcy case. Never lose sight of that.

OUTCOMES I'm sure you wonder what filing bankruptcy would mean for you. Each person's financial situation is unique. It is impossible for me to predict what changes could take place in your life if you decide to file bankruptcy.

Many people feel reduced stress once they know an attorney is working along with them to confront their financial problems. One thing is certain: deciding not to seek legal advice now will guarantee increased stress in your life.

P

PARALEGAL Paralegals can be compared to registered nurses in the medical field. They are often considered the bridge between the professional and the individual who seeks professional services.

In the initial meeting, I would explain that as a paralegal I am entrusted with translating legal terminology into terms that are easily understood. Paralegals also prepare required documents as directed by the attorney.

PARALEGALS CANNOT
GIVE YOU LEGAL ADVICE.

PARALEGALS CANNOT
REPRESENT YOU IN COURT.

I cannot stress these two statements enough. There are times when a paralegal accompanies an attorney to court, but he or she attends only as an aide to the attorney.

Attorneys are trained to accurately predict from a person's beginning point where his or her ending point could be—the *A* and *Z* of the alphabet. Paralegals handle the letters in-between. That includes gathering information, preparing documents, and even calming fears.

PAY STUBS If you received income from a job within the past six months, provide all pay stubs and income records you received for the entire six months to your attorney. This important information is used to perform the Means Test. **Payroll records help determine whether you will file a Chapter 7 or Chapter 13 bankruptcy.**

PENSION INCOME Pension income is received by someone who enrolled in a pension program through their employer, and who now receives that income. The funds in a pension account are usually contributed by an employer over time as a fringe benefit to its employees. **Pension income is added to other types of income when calculating the Means Test.**

PERSONAL PROPERTY Personal property consists of all belongings, cash, financial accounts, and property you own, not including real estate. **Your attorney will ask you to provide a detailed list of this property, along with a yard-sale value for each type of property.**

PREPARE Gather as many of the documents mentioned in the first section of this book as you can before your first meeting with an attorney. Read this entire section so you are familiar with the terms the attorney may use at the appointment. **This book will provide you with the tools necessary to understand the legal advice you receive. This information is vital for making informed decisions about your financial future.**

PRIOR BANKRUPTCY FILING(S) If you filed bankruptcy in the past, it is critical that you tell the attorney about that case at your first meeting. **The date you filed the case, which Chapter you filed, and whether the case was dismissed or discharged will determine the options available to you when filing a new case.** The attorney will work hard for you, and it is important that all information you provide is truthful and complete.

PRIORITY DEBTS Priority debts include debts you owe to the government. They include: past-due taxes, domestic support obligations, wages owed to employees, contributions to employee benefit plans, and claims for death or personal injury to another party.

Q

QUESTIONS The fact-finding mission begins once you hire the attorney, and it will be quite extensive. **The attorney and staff will ask many questions in order to give you the best legal advice possible.** There will be many requests for paperwork and documents. They are all necessary so the office can draft your bankruptcy paperwork. Provide all information as soon as practical so your case can move along smoothly and swiftly.

As stated earlier, you must ask questions of the professionals around you. Much of what you encounter will be foreign to you. **It is important that you fully understand the bankruptcy process and cooperate completely with the attorney and his or her staff.** Make informed decisions and be prepared for the expected outcome of actions taken by an attorney on your behalf.

R

REAFFIRMATION AGREEMENT The attorney will discuss this type of agreement with you if you have a mortgage or car loan. There are other types of loans that might be affected by a reaffirmation agreement, but these two are the most common.

If you agree to sign a Reaffirmation Agreement, you essentially give up the ability to have that loan discharged by the bankruptcy court. **In simple terms if after signing the agreement you lose your job, your health, or your marriage—or you suffer some other life-changing event—you are most likely obligated to repay the debt. You will no longer have protection from the creditor through your bankruptcy.** Ask the attorney how signing this agreement could affect you.

REAL PROPERTY The terms *real property* and *real estate* are interchangeable. In addition to your home or rental property, you may own commercial property or vacant land. **The court requires full disclosure on your part, so be sure to list the details about any real property in your paperwork.**

RENTAL INCOME Some people find it necessary to file bankruptcy because they purchased rental property during better financial times for the extra income, but now can't find paying tenants. The expense of owning the property might exceed income received from rent. Some might also receive rent from a boarder or roommate who shares their home.

You must provide your attorney with a detailed list of all rental income for the past six months. Rental income is taken into account when calculating the Means Test.

REPOSSESSION This action pertains to secured property, such as a vehicle or furniture that can be repossessed if you do not pay the creditor according to the terms of the contract. If you have been notified that you are at risk of losing property to repossession, or you think you might be at risk because your payments are late, meet with an attorney to discuss your options. There are legal remedies that may keep the property safe from repossession.

RESPONSIBILITY Each party who signs a contract has certain responsibilities to uphold. Once either party defaults on his or her contractual responsibilities, the ability to maintain a good working relationship deteriorates. Don't hesitate to seek out professional advice in this situation. It is the responsible thing to do.

RETIREMENT PLANS These assets are included in most bankruptcy cases. Retirement plans have become very common as they are offered by many employers. These plans include 401k, 403b, IRAs, pensions, stock bonuses, profit-sharing accounts, annuities, and accounts that exist due to disability or illness.

The good news is that most retirement plans are now considered exempt property in a bankruptcy case.

S

SCHEDULES The Schedules in a bankruptcy case are individual sections of the paperwork filed with the court. Each Schedule lists specific information. Carefully review and approve the Schedules before you sign them. These Schedules consist of the following:

Schedule A: Real Property
Schedule B: Personal Property
Schedule C: Exemptions
Schedule D: Secured Creditors
Schedule E: Unsecured Priority Creditors
Schedule F: Unsecured Creditors
Schedule G: Executory Contracts and Unexpired Leases
Schedule H: Co-Debtors
Schedule I: Current Income of Individual Debtor(s)
Schedule J: Current Expenditures of Individual Debtor(s)

For detailed explanations of the Schedules, see the "Additional Terms and Concepts" section of this book.

SECURED CREDITORS These creditors retain ownership of property you've purchased until you pay your obligation to them in full. Examples of secured creditors include mortgage companies, the lender on your car loan, and companies that grant home equity loans. These debts are listed on the Schedule D section of your Schedules.

SOCIAL SECURITY INCOME The income you receive from social security or government-issued disability benefits will not be counted toward your **Means Test**. Give the attorney copies of the annual statements showing the amount you receive each month from social security or government-issued disability.

STATEMENT OF FINANCIAL AFFAIRS This section of the bankruptcy paperwork gives the trustee a snapshot of your financial transactions for the past two-to-three years. You need to have the following information available for the attorney to complete this section:

Section 1: Income from employment or operation of business

Section 2: Income other than from employment or operation of business

Section 3: Payments to creditors

Section 4: Suits and administrative proceedings, executions, garnishments, and attachments

Section 5: Repossessions, foreclosures, and returns

Section 6: Assignments and receiverships

Section 7: Gifts

Section 8: Losses

Section 9: Payments related to debt counseling or bankruptcy

Section 10: Other transfers

Section 11: Closed financial accounts

Section 12: Safe-deposit boxes

Section 13: Setoffs

Section 14: Property held for another person

Section 15: Prior address of debtor

Section 16: Spouses and former spouses

Section 17: Environmental information

Section 18: Nature, location and name of business

(Sections nineteen through twenty-five pertain to anyone involved in a business for the past six years. If this is the case for you, continue reading. Otherwise skip to the next topic below.)

Section 19: Books, records and financial statements

Section 20: Inventories

Section 21: Current partners, officers, directors and shareholders

Section 22: Former partners, officers, directors and shareholders

Section 23: Withdrawals from a partnership or distributions by a corporation

Section 24: Tax consolidation group

Section 25: Pension funds

STATEMENT OF INTENTION The Statement of Intention portion of your paperwork lists secured creditors and the corresponding property that secures their loans, such as a home, car, motorcycle, among other property. **The Statement of Intention is a signed document that specifies whether you will retain or surrender each item of secured property.** Review this and all other sections of the bankruptcy paperwork carefully to ensure accuracy.

STRESS I don't have to tell you that the stress caused by financial problems is like no other stress you experience in life. People sometimes experience financial difficulties through no fault of their own. Often there is very little someone can do to improve the situation.

Income and employment are always subject to change. The interest rates on credit cards can rise without your permission or knowledge. **The situations in life that we have little control over tend to stress us out more than the things we can control.**

Filing bankruptcy puts you back in control of your finances, your life, and your future. You owe it to yourself and your family to take the steps that will bring you closer to prosperity and financial health.

STUDENT LOANS Student loans received by you, your spouse, or your children are listed in your bankruptcy. These loans are normally backed by the US government and are not considered dischargeable debts. **You will**

probably have to pay these loans back once the bankruptcy case ends. An attorney will advise you about your student loans.

Bring all student loan documents to the attorney for review. This will ensure that you receive proper advice about whether these debts might be discharged.

<u>SUPPORT</u> Give the attorney copies of all current Support Orders. Court-ordered child or spousal support payments are allowable expenses and will be found on Schedule J of your bankruptcy. These are considered mandatory payments and will be subtracted from gross income amounts.

On the other hand, if you receive child or spousal support you must claim it as income for the Means Test. This income will be listed on the Schedule I section of your case.

T

TAX LIENS If you have ever had a tax lien against your property, you know first-hand that it is a devastating and serious financial matter.

The IRS has a sizeable backlog of work. You aren't notified immediately if you have errors on your latest tax return. Maybe you filed the return but couldn't afford to send the amount due. **There are many situations that put you at risk for the filing of a tax lien.**

If you received notice of a pending tax lien, or a tax lien has been attached to your property, contact an attorney immediately. Find out if filing bankruptcy will allow the lien to be released so you have access to your property again.

TAX RETURNS You are required by bankruptcy law to file your tax returns with the federal and state governments, up to and including the most recent tax year. You must provide your attorney with complete copies of all filed returns for at least the two-year period prior to filing bankruptcy. A copy of your most recent federal income tax return will be supplied to the bankruptcy court and sent to the trustee by your attorney.

TAX TRANSCRIPTS A tax transcript is a document you can request free of charge from the IRS if copies of your federal income tax returns are not available for any reason. **This transcript shows all entries made on your tax return, but is not an actual copy of the return.** The IRS charges a fee to provide actual copies of a tax return you have filed.

TELEPHONE CALLS Most people are harassed by phone calls from their creditors. Collectors will call relentlessly until you break down and send them money. They will stop at nothing to try to force you to pay a debt. They will keep bothering you until you pay the balance, negotiate a lump-sum settlement, or file bankruptcy. Filing bankruptcy might be the best way for you to put an end to these calls. Contact an attorney now to explore your options.

TIME FRAME One of the most frustrating aspects of any legal action is the amount of time it takes to complete the process. Bankruptcy is no different. You can expect a Chapter 7 bankruptcy case to last four to six months. Unusual circumstances could make the case last longer. A Chapter 13 case can last three to five years from the date of filing until completion of the Chapter 13 Debtor's Plan and Discharge.

TRUSTEE The bankruptcy court appoints a trustee to oversee every case. The trustee represents neither you nor the creditors in your case. The trustee works for the court to ensure that the debtor meets all bankruptcy requirements and that all parties in the case are treated fairly.

U

UNEMPLOYMENT Many people experience painful periods of unemployment. This is one of the most stressful situations a hard-working person can face in his or her lifetime. Unemployment is very often the primary reason people file bankruptcy. These individuals paid their bills while they were still employed, and some even contributed to a savings account before losing their jobs.

Unemployment checks amount to less than what someone would receive while working. Unemployment income is factored in the Means Test even though it does not last very long. I know it doesn't sound fair, but it is a painful part of the law.

UNITED STATES CODE The United States Code is the compilation of all federal laws, including those related to bankruptcy. Chapter 7 of the US Code controls the filing of a bankruptcy case that allows a debtor to receive a discharge from most, if not all, unsecured debts.

Chapter 13 of the US Code is a bankruptcy filing that allows someone to repay debts over a period of three to five years and/or keep property worth more than the exemptions allowed by a particular district.

UNITED STATES TRUSTEE The office of the United States Trustee oversees the process of filing a bankruptcy case. This office determines what each Chapter 7 or Chapter 13 trustee considers a violation of certain provisions of the law; it also determines whether property exceeds the exemptions allowed under the law.

<u>UNLISTED DEBTS</u> The rules regarding the discharge of unlisted debts or creditors have been revised since the law changed in 2005. **You must list a creditor on your bankruptcy paperwork in order for that debt to be considered for discharge.** In addition, the information listed for each creditor must include the most current address for receipt of bankruptcy notices by the creditor.

<u>UNSECURED CREDITORS</u> This class includes credit card accounts, unsecured loans, medical bills, utility bills, magazine subscriptions, student loans, deficiency balances from repossessions, dental bills, veterinary services and heating oil bills.

If these unpaid bills are piling up, schedule an appointment to meet with an attorney right now to see if bankruptcy is the right choice for you. Find out how the law pertains to you and how filing could affect your current financial situation. **The process of seeking out sound legal advice and pursuing the proper path for you helps you envision a future without the stress you currently face each day.**

<u>URGENCY</u> It has been my experience that a sense of urgency propels most people into an attorney's office to discuss bankruptcy. **What is the tipping point for your sense of urgency?**

Do you have to be sued by a creditor before you realize that you need to get legal advice?

Does the continuous harassment by creditors have to send you into hysterics every time the phone rings before you make that call to an attorney?

Maybe you have to be down to your last dollar—when you need two dollars just to get through the day—before you call an attorney.

I sincerely hope you will seek the best legal advice you can find as soon as you even suspect you have financial difficulties. If the extra money from working a few hours of overtime each week, or cutting out your daily coffee splurge on the way to work, wouldn't help your situation, it is time to face reality and talk to an attorney.

I know your past is a painful place. Your present is much worse than you could have imagined, and right now the only future you can even think about is making it from today to tomorrow. **Delaying the inevitable will only make the process more painful and costly in the end.**

The future you want for yourself and for your family is in your control. Talk to an attorney openly and honestly about your financial situation. **Make that phone call and take the first step toward a better life.**

<u>UTILITIES</u> No matter where you live, your utility costs have been skyrocketing even as you try hard to control them. **Whether you live in an apartment, with relatives, or in a single-family home, the utility bills you owe when you file bankruptcy can usually be included as unsecured debts.**

What you owe on these bills at the time of filing should be discharged by the bankruptcy court. You can begin with a clean slate with some of these companies once your case is filed. Certain situations will prevent these debts from being discharged.

Ask your attorney what information you must provide so that these utility bills can be included as unsecured creditors in a bankruptcy case. **You may be able to acquire utilities in the future without worrying about paying off those mountainous past-due bills.**

V

VALUATION OF PROPERTY Depending on the type of property you own or have in your possession, the attorney or the court may ask you to obtain a valuation of that property. If you own a home—or any other real estate—the court needs to know the fair market value of that property.

Fine jewelry and firearms will also have to be valued by a certified appraiser if the trustee requests it.

VALUES There are many factors that affect a person's view of bankruptcy and his or her decision to file a bankruptcy case. These factors can be based on family values, religious teachings, work ethic, fears of what people will think, and attitudes about personal responsibility.

Take comfort in knowing that filing bankruptcy is not a crime. It is certainly not a reflection of your personal beliefs or character. **Bankruptcy is nothing more than a legal tool that allows you to address financial situations that are beyond your control. Don't allow fear or an imagined negative stigma shut the door on filing a bankruptcy case.**

VOLUNTARY PETITION The Voluntary Petition is a formal request by the debtor to open a bankruptcy case. The Voluntary Petition contains important personal information such as: the name of the debtor(s), any other names used in the past eight years, address, spouse's name and address (if the case is a joint filing), the estimated number of creditors, the amount owed, and the value of all property. The Chapter of bankruptcy being filed is also listed on the Voluntary Petition.

Information about your attorney is listed on the Voluntary Petition as well. Both you and your attorney must sign the petition. **Review the document very carefully so there are no errors. The bankruptcy court uses this information to enter your case into the database.**

W

WHAT TO DO FIRST When contemplating bankruptcy first do exactly what you are doing now: obtaining information for your first consultation with an attorney. You may need to gather additional items at a later date depending on the complexity of your financial situation. **You are improving your state of mind by taking the first steps toward a positive financial future.**

Relieving the stress in your life will allow you to breathe easier, feel better about yourself, and wake up with a more positive outlook every day. **Keep doing what you are currently doing—taking one informed step at a time.** This journey will eventually lead you to a better place.

X

X-AMINE YOUR BUDGET One of the most positive, long-term effects of filing bankruptcy is that you will develop the skills to create a household budget and stick to it. Prior to gathering the financial information your attorney requested, you probably had no idea how much money was pouring out of your checkbook, or flying off of your debit card, each month.

Of course you were aware of the big bills—mortgage, rent, utilities, and food—before you faced this financial monster. Now you also know how quickly those small purchases add up. They are the expenses that have hidden themselves from view. **Fast-food restaurants and corner coffee shops benefit dramatically from stress and anxiety over money woes.** Those frequent splurges on goodies might make you feel better, but only for a little while.

The money you currently spend without even thinking about it—like that cup of coffee on your way to work—should be deposited instead into a glass jar. You will be able to look at that jar and see your finances grow instead of shrink. When you cash in that jar of change, you can splurge on a new outfit or a dinner for the family. **Once you take a good, hard look at your budget, you will think twice before spending money on unnecessary luxuries. Knowing that you now make better decisions about money will give you a sense of accomplishment.**

Y

YOU ARE THE BOSS Now is the time to reach out to professionals to perform the services you require. **These professionals work for you.** The better you equip yourself with knowledge and information, the better "boss" you will be during the bankruptcy process.

Think of this as one of the most important challenges of your life. **Keep in mind that the bankruptcy process teaches important life lessons that no other experience could have taught you.**

Bankruptcy should be viewed as a fresh start and not a disgrace. Set your mind to making good choices daily for yourself and your family. You will certainly bring about a brighter future.

Z

ZERO TO HERO We've all heard this phrase. When we hear it, we usually think of the nerd with his or her nose in a book who makes it big, or the quiet person in the room who unexpectedly rises to make a moving speech. Sadly I know that the situation you currently find yourself in makes you feel like a zero.

I saw it on the weary faces of many people whose feelings of guilt and shame rose to the surface during our meetings.

I heard it in the strained voices of those on the verge of tears—men and women alike—as they poured their hearts out to me from across the desk.

I sensed it from the anger that had accumulated after years of thinking, "When is it ever going to be easy for me?" The bitter words were finally allowed to audibly escape from imprisonment.

You have to believe that you are not a zero. Your financial situation may have you feeling beaten down, but you don't have to stay down. Making tough choices now and working toward the financial freedom you deserve will have you feeling like a hero again. Just be patient and you will feel good about life before you know it.

IT IS UP TO YOU
TO TAKE THE FIRST STEP.

Now is the time to use this newly acquired knowledge and strength.

STAND UP STRAIGHT,
LOOK AT YOURSELF IN THE MIRROR,

and

IMAGINE THAT YOUR
FINANCIAL HEALTH
HAS ALREADY BEGUN
TO IMPROVE.

Bankruptcy From A To Z

Part Two

THE PATH TO FINANCIAL FREEDOM

FILING BANKRUPTCY AND BEYOND

Fear No More

The first part of this book—"The Path to Financial Hope: Before You File Bankruptcy"—taught you the important questions to ask before choosing an attorney. Now you are ready to pick a legal professional to guide you through the bankruptcy process. Maybe you already found the right attorney for your situation.

Use this book as a companion guide to explain many of the legal terms you will encounter along the way to the final goal of financial freedom. This book does not replace legal advice or the services of a competent attorney. I strongly urge you to hire an attorney immediately so you do not expose yourself to greater financial and legal risk.

You may still be somewhat fearful of filing bankruptcy. I'm sure you have some lingering fears of the unknown. The most common fears shared with me over the years consist of the following:

1. Will I lose my house?
2. Will information about my bankruptcy case be published in the newspaper?
3. Will someone come into my house to see my property?
4. Does hiring an attorney make the harassing telephone calls stop?
5. Do I have to pay back my creditors?
6. Will I have to give up my car(s)?
7. Can the bankruptcy stop a Sheriff's Sale?
8. Can creditors freeze my checking account or take money from my bank accounts?
9. Are bill collectors allowed to call me at work?

10. Does the bankruptcy court send a notice to my employer?
11. Can filing bankruptcy prevent my utilities from being shut off?
12. How do I stop feeling guilty about having to file bankruptcy?
13. If I co-signed for someone on a loan, will the bankruptcy affect his or her credit?
14. Does the Means Test count my gross income or my net income when determining if I am eligible to file a Chapter 7 bankruptcy?
15. How many times do I have to go to court?
16. Will I be approved to file bankruptcy?
17. Can medical bills be included in my bankruptcy?
18. What is the difference between a discharge and a dismissal of a bankruptcy case?
19. What is a Reaffirmation Agreement?
20. Do I have to return the items I purchased on my credit card(s)?
21. Do spouses have to file bankruptcy together or can they file separately?
22. Can I still use some of my credit cards?
23. Do I have to include all of my creditors in a bankruptcy case?

There are additional fears that pertain to life after bankruptcy, such as:

1. How long will the bankruptcy remain on my credit report?
2. Will I ever be able to get credit again?
3. What if my car needs to be replaced after my bankruptcy case is filed?
4. Will creditors begin to call me after the case is over?
5. What happens if I lose my job and I have to file bankruptcy again?
6. Will the bankruptcy filing remain on my credit report if the case is later dismissed?
7. If I am self-employed, can I stay in business after my bankruptcy?
8. How long does the trustee have control over my assets?

Answers to these and all other questions will be provided by your attorney. Just remember to ask the questions. Feel free to use this as a handbook so you can jot the answers down. **Be well-informed along the way, and you will** definitely be able to make smart decisions—not just now, but in the future as well.

In the following pages, you will find the necessary information to dispel any lingering fears. Let's work together to build your courage to move beyond this period of financial distress.

Overcome the Guilt

It was always a challenge for me to confront the pain of guilt I saw in clients' faces. I wanted to point to the path that would eventually move them beyond their self-imposed shame into a positive sense of well-being.

Someone facing bankruptcy often experiences an overwhelming sense of guilt. Our society calls for personal honesty and integrity, and that expectation has been indelibly implanted into each of us. Religious beliefs and individual heritage also impose tremendous burdens on those unable to honor their financial commitments. Historically society has turned an inability to repay debts into a reflection of personal character.

I remember a time when those who didn't honor their debts faced scorn or, even worse, public disgrace. More recently families unable to make mortgage payments and other obligations have experienced nightmare images of going to debtor's prison or worse.

As times have changed concerning borrowing, so have attitudes about repayment. When reviewing clients' credit card statements, I could easily see they were using these all-too-convenient pieces of plastic to feed their families and clothe their children. The bank or credit card company surely wouldn't allow a credit limit to be higher than what a person could repay—or would they?

Considering interest rates are sky-high, and contracts for credit are very one-sided in favor of the lender, many people have fallen victim to powerful lenders. The substantial debts they incur could never be repaid, no matter how long they live.

When you think about your situation and attempt to figure out how you got to this point, factor in the reality that credit card interest can be compared to the rates that loan sharks charge. **It might be your responsibility to repay "just" or "fair" debt, but you shouldn't be beaten down for the rest of your life by unfair interest rates. Certain predatory lending practices could almost be considered criminal in nature.**

Many believed banks and credit card companies wouldn't lend them more money, or increase their credit limits, if they didn't qualify financially to repay the higher amounts. Some told me even though they didn't request an increase, companies raised the limits on their credit cards. Those individuals truly thought they could pay for those purchases over a period of time. Those increased limits meant they could now buy that bigger refrigerator or the new car they saw on television. **After all, the banks hire professionals don't they? They evaluate credit risk for a living. They should know best, right?**

There was a time when that was true. Years ago I worked for a major automobile credit company when borrowing standards were tough. It was difficult to be approved for a car loan, not to mention an unsecured credit card. Those times are long gone. Lenders have evolved into companies that want balances to linger on for years because of the high interest rates. **Banks are more profitable when you don't pay off your balances in a short period of time. They certainly don't mind if you pay a little late so they can charge past-due fees.** Even without seeing your credit card statements, I can tell the balances on your credit card accounts will outlive you because of the extraordinarily high interest rates.

If your attorney has advised you to file bankruptcy, you owe it to yourself to make use of the protection under the bankruptcy laws to get out from under that growing pile of debt. Each day that goes by, creditors add interest and fees to purchases made long ago. That money should stay in your pocket so you can take care of yourself and your loved ones. The credit companies already received more than their fair share.

If you can't pay for basic necessities while you attempt to pay off those credit cards, filing bankruptcy might allow you to take control over your finances and obligations. You will surely make smarter decisions in the future and live a healthier and less stressful life.

The lenders have to answer to regulators and the government, and you know who you have to answer to according to your beliefs. **Do what is right for you and your family.** Look at this process as a financial decision that should greatly enhance the quality of your life.

> **Take responsibility**
> **for the part you played,**
> **and then let go of the guilt.**

Learn the lessons you need to learn, and trust you are making sound, legal decisions to move on with the rest of your life. Don't allow others to pass judgment on you. You would be surprised to see how many others have walked in your shoes.

Step into the future with self-respect and purpose. Don't worry about what others may think. **Your mental health and emotional well-being are so much more important than being hard on yourself.**

> **Be prepared for your life to change –**
> **for the better.**

Financial Freedom

Each step you take will move you toward your goals of financial freedom and a brighter future. If you are looking for an overnight sensation, you will have to look for something other than bankruptcy. Filing bankruptcy and moving beyond serious financial struggles takes time. The stress you feel now won't disappear immediately, and your future won't look bright right away. Stay positive, and remain on the right track. **If you are patient, focused, and alert, you will come through this crisis better off than you were when you faced financial despair.**

It would be impossible to include all of the legal terms you might encounter, so I have listed the most common ones to get you started. Some terms appear in more than one section. Those particular terms will arise most often. I have listed them more frequently for that reason. Seek detailed explanations of those terms in the next part of this book.

I realize that reading this whole book immediately may not be practical. An entire section may be more than you can digest in one sitting. **Depending on the urgency of your situation, begin by looking up the individual terms you need to know right now. You can read the rest of the material when you have more time and the world around you relaxes a bit.** I intend this material to function as your guide. You will use it the way that is best for you.

A brighter future awaits you. This book will lead you to it. Now let's continue the journey together.

And again
the only place to start
is with the letter *A*

THE PATH TO FINANCIAL FREEDOM
Additional Terms And Concepts

A

APPRAISALS Your attorney may ask you to have your real estate appraised to determine its actual worth at the time you file your case. There will be an extra cost to hire someone to do the appraisal, but in the long run it will be money well spent. The trustee in your case will be aware of home values in your general area, but will not know the actual condition and value of your home. **A recent written appraisal performed by a certified, reputable appraiser will support what you state as the value of your property.**

The equity in your property helps determine if you must pay any money back to creditors. **If your attorney asks for an appraisal, get one immediately.** The attorney can recommend someone for this valuable service.

ASSETS The value of your assets will be determined during the bankruptcy process. **This figure includes the value of all real estate you own added to the value of your personal property.** Real estate includes the home you live in and any other properties you own. Your personal property includes, among other items: cars, clothing, time shares, financial accounts, and furniture.

The trustee controls your assets during the bankruptcy process. That means you cannot list your home for sale, sell any real estate or personal property, or even purchase or sell any vehicles without first discussing the matter with your attorney. The trustee must approve many of these transactions.

You must disclose to the court any purchase or sale of property you were involved in two to three years prior to filing bankruptcy. It will be necessary to provide copies of real estate settlement sheets so the trustee can confirm the details of these transactions. Make sure to give copies to your attorney before filing your case; they may affect the legal advice you receive.

B

BILLS Bankruptcy law requires you to list all of your debts when you file your case. You will have to pay debts back if they are not properly listed on your paperwork.

Give your attorney the names, addresses, account numbers, and balances for all your creditors as soon as you can. You will pay additional fees if the attorney has to research any information you have forgotten or intentionally omitted.

Double-check all information on the list of creditors your attorney prepares. Attorneys and their staff sometimes make mistakes. It is your responsibility to verify the accuracy of any paperwork you sign.

BUSINESS INCOME AND EXPENSES Many people who file personal bankruptcy own and operate small businesses. It is possible to file a bankruptcy case even if you are self-employed. Compile at least twelve months' worth of business accounting records—including gross income, categorized expenses, and net income—before meeting with an attorney.

If you are self-employed, copies of tax returns for the previous three years are required so the attorney can determine which Chapter of bankruptcy code is appropriate for you.

You must give your attorney complete information to receive the most effective legal advice and service available to you.

C

CHAPTER 7 BANKRUPTCY After qualifying to file a Chapter 7 bankruptcy by passing the Means Test (i.e., your gross income is below the amount set by the office of the US Trustee), you usually have immediate protection from any creditors attempting to collect on your unsecured debts once your case is filed.

By filing Chapter 7, you normally will not have to pay these debts off at any time. These balances include personal loans, credit card bills, medical bills, and utility bills, among many other types of debt. **In order to keep your house and car, you must continue to pay the monthly payments on these accounts until they are paid in full. They are considered secured debts.**

You may be asked to sign a Reaffirmation Agreement with a creditor when you have a mortgage or car loan. **Ask your attorney how these agreements could affect your rights, especially if your circumstances change in the future**. You could lose your job, get a divorce, or suffer from an unforeseen illness that might affect your ability to pay after signing a Reaffirmation Agreement. There is a period of time when you are permitted to rescind a Reaffirmation Agreement. Get sound legal advice on this important matter.

Discuss any liens on your property with the attorney so you can avoid unnecessary stress and expense in the future. The disposition of these liens should be handled during your bankruptcy case. Often a debtor intends to sell his or her house sometime in the future, and Chapter 7 bankruptcy allows him or her to ride out the storm. **There is the distinct possibility of losing a** qualified buyer in a tough real estate market if a lien exists on your real estate. Expert legal advice is important in this situation.

CHAPTER 7 TRUSTEE The bankruptcy court assigns a trustee to every case that is filed. The trustee does not represent you or the creditors in your case. **Trustees are appointed by the court to verify that your case conforms to bankruptcy law.** The trustee also confirms that none of your assets should be sold to pay off your debts. Very often, trustees are attorneys who understand the ins and outs of representing people in bankruptcy cases because they still work as private attorneys in the field. **The trustee also determines if you are telling the truth about your income and assets.**

The trustee represents the federal government for the duration of your case. Always be respectful toward the trustee and all court officials. You will appear before the trustee when you attend the mandatory Meeting of Creditors along with your attorney. The bankruptcy court controls your assets and liabilities until your case is closed (and even for a period of time afterward).

Honesty is the best policy from the very beginning of your case. A Chapter 7 trustee has overseen hundreds—possibly thousands—of cases over time. It is easy for a trustee to spot dishonest statements and hidden assets. **You will be subject to losing property and legal action if you lie to the court about your finances.**

CHAPTER 13 BANKRUPTCY This type of bankruptcy is appropriate for some debtors for the following reasons: their gross income is **above the Means Test amount allowed for their household size,** even after subtracting all allowable expenses; they are so far **behind on their mortgage payments** that they need three to five years to catch up; or **their assets are in excess of the exemptions they are allowed to claim** before having to sell property to pay creditors. Also if you **filed a Chapter 7 case within eight years** of filing bankruptcy again, it may be necessary to file Chapter 13.

Filing a Chapter 13 bankruptcy case requires you to make a regular payment to the Chapter 13 trustee for the length of your case. The amount of this payment is determined by how much you owe to creditors who filed approved claims with the court, and what the guidelines of the court determine as your disposable income.

IMPORTANT! When you file a Chapter 13 bankruptcy and you have a mortgage on a home that you wish to keep, you must continue to pay your normal monthly mortgage payments on time. You must also make payments on all secured debts (such as car loans). Lastly your monthly payment of the Chapter 13 Debtor's Plan must be made on time.

Be realistic about the amount you are able to pay each month when deciding if you can keep your home. If you don't make enough money to cover the required monthly payments—along with paying for utilities, child care, food, and the necessities of life—it may be time to let your house go and move on with your life. Speak openly with your attorney about your ability to keep your home. Be prepared to accept some difficult news—it may be necessary so that you can move on to a brighter future.

<u>CHAPTER 13 DEBTOR'S PLAN</u> This document is filed with the court in all Chapter 13 cases. It outlines the amount that a Chapter 13 debtor must pay to the trustee each month for a period of three to five years. It lists the court-approved claims of all creditors that must be paid out of funds received from the debtor.

If you file a Chapter 13 case, the court takes the following into account: your disposable income (determined by federal guidelines), the balances on accounts owed to creditors who have filed approved claims (requests for payment), and the amount of the commission to be paid to the trustee's office for the administration of your case. A portion of your attorney fees can be included in the Chapter 13 Debtor's Plan so you pay less up front to the attorney when filing your case. You send the plan payments to the Chapter 13 Trustee and the trustee's office will send your attorney the balance of his or her fee. Ask your attorney if this option is available to you.

<u>CIVIL LITIGATION</u> Make your attorney aware of any lawsuits immediately. Short of filing bankruptcy, there are no real protections from creditors collecting on judgments. Once you have filed, your attorney can provide your bankruptcy case information directly to creditors who have sued you. All collection efforts should stop as soon as those creditors are notified individually. Any companies that have threatened to shut off your utilities should also be notified as soon as your case is filed. Most attorneys charge a nominal fee for this service, but it will halt legal actions quickly.

<u>CO-DEBTOR</u> (pronounced "co-detter") A person jointly obligated to pay a debt is a co-debtor. If both you and your spouse have signed on a loan or credit card, you are co-debtors. If you co-signed for anyone else on a loan, you are a co-debtor on that obligation.

A co-debtor is responsible for repaying a debt if the other party does not repay it for any reason. Creditors will go after anyone they can pursue legally to get their money back.

For example, if your parent co-signed for you and you don't repay the debt on time, the creditor will certainly harass and annoy that parent through phone calls, letters or personal visits. You should inform anyone you co-signed with or for, or anyone who has co-signed for you, that you are filing bankruptcy. The filing could also affect the co-signer's credit report or credit score.

<u>COMMITMENT PERIOD</u> The commitment period is the time period that a Chapter 13 bankruptcy lasts. This is determined when the court confirms which debts must be repaid and how much disposable income is available to pay past-due amounts. The commitment period is usually between three and five years.

The attorney fees to file Chapter 13 are generally higher than for a Chapter 7 case because the attorney monitors your case for a three-to-five-year period. Know the proposed duration of your Chapter 13 Debtor's Plan before you file your case.

<u>CONFIRMATION OF CHAPTER 13 PLAN</u> The Chapter 13 Debtor's Plan (Plan) should be filed with the court when your case is initially filed. If it is not filed at that time, the court automatically sets a deadline for the document to be filed, which at the time of this writing is just fourteen days. The court will routinely file a Motion to Dismiss a case in order to preserve its right to address time-limit violations. A hearing date is set for the confirmation, or approval, of your Plan.

Review the Plan extensively with your attorney before it is filed with the court. The amount you must pay to the Chapter 13 Trustee each month is contained in the document, along with the schedule of distribution of those funds to approved claims of creditors. This payment is in addition to your mortgage and car loan payments. The Chapter 13 Debtor's Plan requires your signature. Do not sign any paperwork unless you understand and agree with the information contained in it.

It is likely that you will file at least one Amended Plan before the final document is confirmed by the court. Always understand what you are signing. You are obligated to fulfill the terms of the Chapter 13 Debtor's Plan. This document ultimately affects your property and disposable income.

CONVERSION TO A DIFFERENT CHAPTER OF BANKRUPTCY It is possible to file a case under Chapter 7 and then convert to Chapter 13 at a later time. You can also convert from Chapter 13 to Chapter 7.

Conversion to Chapter 7 can be useful in situations where income levels have changed dramatically since the filing of the bankruptcy case, or eight years have passed since filing a previous Chapter 7 case that ended with a discharge.

A debtor may also find it impossible to keep up with Chapter 13 payments for various reasons, or he or she may no longer wish to keep his or her home. If you and your attorney think it is best to convert your case, you need to review and sign paperwork to notify the court of the conversion.

Your attorney will charge additional fees and costs for the conversion process. Additional documents must be filed with the court. Another court appearance is necessary for you and the attorney since a new Meeting of Creditors will be scheduled before the newly-appointed trustee. Ask about the additional costs before you convert your case.

CREDIT RE-ESTABLISHMENT Most people think they will never be able to get a mortgage, personal loan, or credit card again if they file bankruptcy. This is not usually true. On the other hand, some clients have actually asked me how they can get a new credit card even before they have completed the bankruptcy process. The latter scenario represents someone who has not learned anything from going through the ordeal of bankruptcy.

You might be granted credit after a bankruptcy case has concluded. Just keep in mind that you might have to pay higher interest rates or have to wait awhile before borrowing money again. Every lending institution has its own policies and qualifications in place for borrowing money, especially for applicants who have filed bankruptcy.

A Discharge of Debtor Order is provided by the court when your case has concluded. Take a copy of the Order with you to the car dealership when you need to purchase a vehicle. Some banks consider people with a discharged bankruptcy better credit risks than people who have slow credit and have not filed bankruptcy. **You cannot file a Chapter 7 bankruptcy again for a period of eight years after receiving your discharge.** For that reason you may be a better credit risk than someone with slow credit.

As a Chapter 13 debtor, you must receive permission from the trustee before buying a car, replacing a current vehicle, refinancing your mortgage, or selling your property. These transactions are under the control of the trustee until your Chapter 13 Debtor's Plan has been paid in full, and your case has been discharged.

D

DEBT MANAGEMENT This term refers to planning out the liability, or debt portion of your budget. You have been in control of the management of your debt until now. **When you file a bankruptcy case, the court becomes involved in the debt management process.** You cannot acquire new loans, sell your home, or even pay off credit cards without the court being involved. This includes loans made to you by your family or friends. Discuss these types of debts with your attorney immediately.

DISCHARGE After completing the bankruptcy process, either Chapter 7 or 13, the goal is to receive a discharge of your debts. This means that creditors will no longer be allowed to collect on those debts unless the court has determined that a debt is non-dischargeable. **You must ask your attorney if any of your debts could be considered non-dischargeable.**

If you charged on a credit card or incurred new debt within a month or so of filing bankruptcy, the creditor can file a Complaint to Object to Discharge concerning that debt. The Complaint only pertains to the money that you owe that particular creditor.

There are other situations that could prevent you from receiving a discharge in a bankruptcy case. Ask your attorney detailed questions about bankruptcy discharge and how it will affect the balances you owe your individual creditors.

DISMISSAL Sometimes a bankruptcy case is dismissed by the court, and the debtor no longer has protection under the bankruptcy laws. The case is then closed by the court. A case can be dismissed if: you or your attorney do not provide all information requested by the court or trustee in a timely manner, a Chapter 13 debtor stops making his or her plan payments or it is determined that the debtor has committed fraud or abused bankruptcy laws.

Many clients treat Motions to Dismiss nonchalantly, just as they had previously treated collection calls from their creditors. Do not ignore any notices from the court, especially if you don't understand the meaning of them. All notices are important, but if the words Motion or Order appear anywhere on a document, it is extremely important.

IF THE COURT FILES A MOTION TO DISMISS YOUR CASE, YOU OR YOUR ATTORNEY MUST RESPOND TO THE MOTION WITHIN A SPECIFIC PERIOD OF TIME OR YOUR CASE WILL BE DISMISSED.

Meet with your attorney without delay to determine what steps you must take to resolve any issues the court has with your case. Your financial future depends on it.

DISPOSABLE INCOME When you file bankruptcy, your attorney will provide paperwork to the court that lists your income and expenses. This information is found both in the Schedule I (income) and Schedule J (expense) section of your paperwork. The federal government sets guidelines for these amounts by using the IRS standards for your area. **Any income that remains after paying all of your allowable expenses is called disposable income.** This figure is especially important in a Chapter 13 bankruptcy because it is one factor used to determine how much will be paid into the Chapter 13 Debtor's Plan.

In some instances, if your disposable income is higher than allowed by law in a Chapter 7 case, the trustee may file paperwork with the court requesting that an equivalent portion of your property be sold to pay creditors. The trustee would then request to change your case to an asset case by filing a Motion with the court.

Ask the attorney specific questions about your disposable income. You don't want to lose property or pay money to the trustee if you can avoid it.

Even though you probably have a negative balance in your checkbook most of the time, the court may not allow you to claim all of your expenses. **The law allows the trustee to look very closely at your budget to determine if you spend your money on necessities.** Your attorney will know which expenses you will be allowed to claim in your case.

E

EQUITY The equity in your property is the difference between what your property (house, car, household goods, etc.) is worth and how much you owe on that property. If you have a house worth $200,000 and you owe $180,000 on it, you have positive equity of $20,000. As is common now, you may owe more than your home is worth. For example, if your home is worth $180,000 but you owe $200,000 on it, you have negative equity of $20,000.

The equity in your property is one factor that determines whether the trustee recommends to the court that your property should be sold to pay your debts.

This part of bankruptcy law is quite confusing. Actually, the way equity is handled can even differ from district to district and trustee to trustee. A good attorney will know how the trustee assigned to your case will treat the equity in your property.

EXECUTORY CONTRACT Executory contracts are more commonly known as leases. These contracts allow you to possess and control property, but do not give you a vested interest or ownership in the property. If you rent an apartment or house, lease a car, or have a vacation timeshare, you must provide that information to your attorney.

These debts are listed on the Schedule G portion of your paperwork. Your attorney may also list these debts on Schedule D, E, or F, depending on the type of creditor—secured, priority, or unsecured.

You should also include on your bankruptcy the amount the dealer has calculated as your outstanding balance when you return a leased vehicle. Show your attorney the lease contract and all letters or bills from the leasing company.

F

FINANCIAL MANAGEMENT COURSE This is a mandatory requirement after filing either a Chapter 7 or Chapter 13 bankruptcy. It is referred to as the Financial Management Course. Your attorney will give you the contact information for the court-approved provider used by his or her firm. You can also review the list of approved providers at the US Trustee's website.

The cost for this course differs from provider to provider. Depending on the provider you choose it can be completed either online or by telephone, and in some languages other than English. If your income falls below a certain level, there may be no charge for this course. If you do not complete this requirement within forty-five days of the date your Meeting of Creditors was originally scheduled, the bankruptcy court will close your case without granting a discharge. In other words you would have gone through the entire bankruptcy process for nothing. You would not receive any protection from the debts you owed. Do not forget to complete this mandatory requirement.

I strongly suggest to debtors that they complete this course prior to attending the Meeting of Creditors. Not only does completing it relieve your mind that you fulfilled the requirement, it demonstrates to the trustee that you are serious about your obligations as a debtor in bankruptcy.

FRAUDULENT TRANSFERS If you have transferred property such as a home, car, or bank account into someone else's name within the past few years, the court will request details about the transaction. In some instances people who filed bankruptcy in the past were dishonest and attempted to hide assets or otherwise prevent creditors from seizing assets through legal action. The trustee is trained to spot these fraudulent transactions.

A fraudulent transfer on the part of a debtor is considered a violation of bankruptcy law. When the transfer is discovered it triggers actions by both the US Trustee and the Chapter 7 or 13 Trustee. **Any fraudulent transfers of property that violate bankruptcy law will be corrected by appropriate means.** That includes requiring the debtor to sell the asset and then pay the court or affected creditors directly. The court can even reverse real estate transactions that have taken place in certain situations. **Fraudulent transfers don't happen often, but often enough for the court to be on the lookout for them.**

<u>FULL DISCLOSURE</u> This term means that as the debtor **you swear to provide** *all* **financial information requested by your attorney and the court** during the bankruptcy process. **In addition, the information you provide is expected to be true and correct.** If assets are uncovered by the court that you did not disclose on the paperwork, your case will be negatively affected. You could lose property or be required to pay money back to creditors, either immediately or over time.

You must tell your attorney everything about your financial situation or suffer the consequences.

Attorneys are officers of the court, and they are obligated by law to divulge the information you give them. You cannot request that this information remain "just between us." The 2005 law puts your attorney in the position of verifying the information you provide and determining reasonably if any information is missing or fraudulent. **Efforts to withhold information or knowingly provide incorrect information will be punished by the federal bankruptcy court.**

G

GARNISHMENT Creditors can take certain actions to collect on a judgment. If a creditor received a judgment against you, and you have not made arrangements to pay off the judgment, the creditor may attempt to garnish your wages. You must tell your attorney immediately if you have any judgments entered against you for any reason.

Just because a creditor has not acted on a judgment for an extended period of time—or you don't get letters from them anymore—doesn't mean that your assets won't be frozen or your paycheck won't be garnished. Until you convince your bank and the creditor (or their attorney) that you don't owe the money, you will have no access to funds that have been garnished or frozen. Even if you have bills due and need to buy food for your family, you cannot access that money. **Any legal actions you face must be brought to the attention of your attorney immediately.**

When you meet with an attorney for the first time, you should bring any paperwork concerning lawsuits filed against you. If the attorney has to contact the court to obtain this information directly, you will most likely be billed for the extra time expended by his or her staff to do so.

GOOD FAITH The bankruptcy court reviews your financial history for approximately the previous three years. The trustee might also ask what circumstances led to the bankruptcy filing.

Some people file bankruptcy as a tactic to stall lawsuits with no intention of completing the case. They file bankruptcy just to keep the wolves at bay for the short term, but that only works until the case gets dismissed. They are trying to buy time, but in the long run it can be a very costly maneuver.

If the court determines that a case was not filed by a debtor in *good faith*, it affects not only the outcome of that case, but also the ability to receive permission from the court to file any future cases.

H

HEALTH INSURANCE PREMIUMS Many debtors pay some, if not all, of their own health insurance premiums. These amounts are listed on the pay stubs of people who contribute toward their premiums for employer-provided health insurance. **This is an allowable expense on the Means Test.** If you do not initially qualify to file a Chapter 7 bankruptcy, make sure that your attorney has included these costs with your expenses. **Provide actual figures to your attorney for any premiums that you pay toward health insurance so you can claim this expense in your bankruptcy.**

HOUSEHOLD GOODS Your household goods are considered personal property. These items include furniture, televisions, appliances, clothing, and anything else that could be found in the household goods section of a department store. **Even if someone gave you the item as a gift, you must include it on your paperwork.**

There are generous exemptions for personal property because the bankruptcy court wants you to be able to keep items necessary to have a decent life. It would benefit no one if filing bankruptcy left people homeless and destitute. The court may not seem fair and reasonable to you, but it determines what property is necessary for an individual or family according to standards set by the IRS.

The debts normally discharged in bankruptcy are those incurred through purchases of personal property. **It stands to reason that you would expect to live within the limits set by the court for a short time in exchange** for the opportunity to come out of bankruptcy with little or no debt. If individuals were permitted to keep extravagant amounts of property without paying for it in the end, the bankruptcy process would not be fair to anyone.

I

INCOME EXCLUSIONS Some types of income generally excluded from the Means Test include: social security, social security- disability, payments received by victims of crime or terrorism, and income of a non-filing spouse who lives apart from you or who is legally separated from you.

INDIVIDUAL RETIREMENT ACCOUNTS IRAs, as they are commonly known and tax-qualified retirement funds are exempt under federal bankruptcy exemptions or state law. There is an exemption limit for most IRAs. Check with your attorney to determine if your IRA will be considered exempt in your bankruptcy.

IRS STANDARDS The IRS is part of the federal government. Bankruptcy cases are filed in the federal court system. The standard amounts for income, exemptions, housing expenses, utilities, food, transportation, and vehicle costs are set by IRS guidelines. Your attorney can explain how these standards will affect the outcome of your Means Test.

J

JUDGE Your residential address determines the district where your case is filed. **A judge is assigned to your bankruptcy case at the time of filing.** Each judge handles a particular district within the bankruptcy court, depending on geographical location.

The attorney you hire must be aware of how that judge normally rules on matters relevant to your case. If the attorney doesn't know much about the judge or his or her published legal Opinions, it would be best to find another attorney. Some attorneys only dabble in bankruptcy law and don't have the knowledge necessary to properly handle your case.

How well the attorney knows the rulings of the judge in your particular district could easily come into play in your case. If the attorney you interview doesn't file a large number of bankruptcies, it may be smart to continue the search for a qualified attorney.

JUDICIAL LIEN When you lose a lawsuit and the other party receives a judgment against you for a certain amount of money, that party files a lien against your property. Except in the case of judicial liens that secure a domestic support obligation (past-due child or spousal support), you can generally file a Motion to Avoid a Lien that has been filed against you.

After you file bankruptcy, your property is protected from creditors up to the amount of your allowable exemption on that property. **If liens are filed against protected (exempt) property, your attorney can file the paperwork necessary to invalidate the lien.** Attorneys will charge an additional fee to file this Motion and to attend court on your behalf. It may be worth the additional expense if the lien is for a significant amount or if the existing lien would hinder the sale of property.

Ask as many questions as needed to completely understand the process before giving your attorney the green light to file a Motion to Avoid Lien. You are personally responsible for all actions or paperwork filed in your case. There is an additional attorney fee to file the Motion and no guarantee that the Motion will be granted by the court.

K

KEEP YOUR STRESS LEVEL DOWN I cannot emphasize enough that knowledge of the process prior to filing bankruptcy will greatly diminish the stress you feel during the bankruptcy.

The best side effect of going through bankruptcy is that less of your energy will be wasted on stress, and more energy can be focused on improving your life.

You have taken an important step by reading this book. The information contained here, and the legal advice provided by your attorney, will help guide your way and ease your worries immeasurably.

KNOWLEDGE You have heard over and over that knowledge is a major key to success. At this time in your life, a successful bankruptcy case is the most important focus of your attention. **The more knowledgeable you become now about credit terms and financial matters, the more successful you will be when your case reaches its conclusion.** Take advantage of the professionals around you, and learn all you can. **Your financial future depends on it.**

L

LAWSUITS When the new bankruptcy law was enacted in 2005, the number of lawsuits filed against debtors rose dramatically. **Unsecured creditors can now sometimes receive funds from a debtor in either a Chapter 13 or Chapter 7 Asset case.** Credit card companies have pushed lawsuits through county court systems in record numbers.

Prior to 2005 creditors would have written off uncollected, outstanding balances because they had little or no chance of recovering the money under bankruptcy law. Those same creditors are now filing civil lawsuits and receiving judgments mainly against debtors who are delinquent on their credit card payments. These creditors might also be collectors hired by providers who rendered medical services to a debtor or family member.

Many past-due accounts are sold to companies that pay pennies on the dollar so they can attempt to collect those balances. **If you receive a notice that you have been sued, meet with an experienced attorney immediately.** If you have hired an attorney, bring a copy of any legal notice or lawsuit to his or her office as soon as you receive it.

LIEN A lien is a document filed with the civil court that places a security interest in your property for the benefit of the creditor. When a lien has been placed on your property, you are not free to sell it without first paying off the lien. Many clients do not realize they have a lien on their property until they sell their home. The title company for the buyer performs a lien search, and this is when most liens are discovered.

A creditor is required to send notice of a lien to the person who owns the property affected by the lien. Sadly many people do not pay attention to their mail, even when it concerns a lawsuit. Denial of the situation creates more problems than they could ever anticipate. Your attorney must be told about any lawsuit, old or new, so that it is properly handled in your bankruptcy.

LIEN AVOIDANCE MOTION If you have a lien securing any of your debts, your attorney should discuss a Lien Avoidance Motion with you. There will be an additional fee to file this Motion, and possibly a court appearance for both you and your attorney. **Depending on what property is affected and the amount of the lien, it may be beneficial to file the Motion so you do not lose property in the future.**

M

MARITAL PROBLEMS If you are married, you have probably noticed a strain on your relationship caused by money problems. Many people who file bankruptcy also end up going through a divorce because of their financial situation. It is quite common that the stress caused by financial problems can weaken the family structure.

Many people who address their money problems and then decide to file bankruptcy are able to save their relationships. Some couples even find that their marriage is stronger afterward. Have an honest discussion with your spouse to see if solving the money problems might also lead to solving your marital problems.

MEANS TEST The Means Test became a mandatory provision of bankruptcy law in 2005. This test is used to calculate a debtor's Current Monthly Income (CMI), as the Bankruptcy Code refers to it. Your attorney and the court use the Means Test to determine if a presumption of abuse arises and if you qualify to file a Chapter 7 case.

In simple terms, if you have the means to do so you will be required to pay back at least some of your debts. If you are fortunate enough to qualify to file a Chapter 7 bankruptcy, you should not be required to pay money to creditors who do not hold a secured interest in your property.

Even if you qualify under the Means Test as a Chapter 7 debtor, you can decide to file Chapter 13 instead if it allows you to save your home or other property. This is especially helpful if you are past-due on your mortgage payments. Ask your attorney if your delinquent payments can be paid back to the mortgage company through a Chapter 13 Debtor's Plan over a period of three to five years. Many people have found this to be the best solution to their financial problems.

MEDIAN INCOME Median income figures are determined for each area of the country by the IRS. These figures are used by the bankruptcy court to set the maximum income for a particular family size. Based on this information, you may initially qualify as a Chapter 7 debtor. If your income is above the Chapter 7 threshold, your attorney can perform a more detailed Means Test to see if allowable expenses reduce your income sufficiently to allow you to file a Chapter 7 bankruptcy.

You can find the most recent Median Income figures at http://www.justice. gov/ust. Click on the link for median income and find your state on the tables listed there. Your household size will be one of the factors used to determine if your income is below or above the median income for your area. It will help determine if you file a Chapter 7 or Chapter 13 bankruptcy.

MODIFICATION AGREEMENT You can request to enter into a Modification Agreement with a creditor. This agreement allows both parties to agree to modify the terms of a debt, normally a mortgage. The process can be very time-consuming, and might seem complicated, but it could be well worth the effort.

You will be asked to provide many documents, just like you did when you first applied for the mortgage. Lenders have special departments set up just to review these documents and determine if a particular mortgage can be modified. The process is quite lengthy and does not always result in an approval. Nonetheless, I've always said to clients that they won't know if it will work for them until they try. Ask your attorney if this process could be beneficial to you.

If you request a Modification Agreement through your mortgage company, provide all documents requested by them as soon as possible. If you send the information by mail, send them in a way that requires a signature. You can then prove when they were received by the company. It is important to follow up on the status of your request for a modification since many people are requesting these transactions. Do not allow your request to be overlooked.

Your attorney must send written permission to the creditor allowing them to contact you directly and only for the purpose of negotiating a Modification Agreement. This preserves your legal representation for all portions of your bankruptcy case.

Numerous people have been successful in their requests for Modification Agreements. **Even though the mortgage company will negotiate with you directly during this process, you must always have your attorney review any agreements or documents prior to signing them.**

<u>MOTIONS</u> **A Motion under bankruptcy law is a formal request filed with the court asking for a specific action to take place.** Motions a debtor might file include: Motion to Extend Automatic Stay, Motion to Value Secured Property, Motion to Approve Realtor, Motion to Sell Real Property Free and Clear of All Liens, and many others.

When your attorney files a Motion on your behalf, there is usually an additional charge. Motions not only require documents to be drafted and filed, a court appearance by you and/or your attorney may be necessary as well. More often than not, you must appear in court with your attorney.

Since you have probably never gone through this process before, you must ask your attorney specifics about the process and what is required of you. **Don't be afraid to ask all the questions necessary so you fully understand the Motion and all possible outcomes.** Court proceedings are never completely predictable, so you must understand the likelihood of your Motion being granted or denied prior to filing the Motion.

Legal advice concerning Motions can be very complex and somewhat confusing. It is very important that you receive reliable advice before you instruct your attorney to move forward with filing any Motion in your bankruptcy.

N

NET INCOME Your net income is determined by adding all of your income sources and then subtracting taxes and allowable deductions. Sources of income include your job, any part-time employment, your spouse's income, employer disability payments, and more. Certain types of income—such as social security—are generally exempt from the Means Test.

Many clients think that the court only takes their net income into account when calculating the Means Test, but the process actually begins with your gross income. Review the entry for "Gross Income" in this section of the book to see some examples.

The court only allows specific expenses to be deducted from your gross income for the purpose of filing bankruptcy. You must supply a list of all of your expenses and deductions to the attorney so they can be considered when subtracting expenses from your gross income. The attorney will then determine your net income. **The attorney will know what deductions qualify under the law.**

NEW OUTLOOK My hope for you is that you develop a new outlook on your financial future during the bankruptcy process. **You will learn new concepts about finances and your budget from the financial management course.** It might feel like a chore to complete the task, but I am sure you'll find that you will gain knowledge and discipline after you complete the course.

You must work to ensure that your future is better than your past. I know you can do it! Many clients expressed a sense of freedom after filing bankruptcy because they learned they could live without using their credit cards. **The process restored a feeling of control they had lost when they faced massive debt and the inability to repay it.**

Changing how you feel about filing bankruptcy will allow you to improve your self-esteem. **Bankruptcy is basically no more than a financial decision on your part, and it is allowable by law.** The odds are that it will propel you to a better way of life. Most of our clients would never have lived long enough to pay off the debts they owed.

Your improved financial health prepares you for a brighter future. It begins with this fresh start.

NEW START I always approached a new bankruptcy case with the mindset that the process would be a fresh start for the person and not a disgrace. I want you to adopt that mindset as well.

NON-DISCHARGEABILITY Most of your debts should be discharged by the bankruptcy court. There are certain debts that are not dischargeable. They include the following: specific taxes owed to the government; most education loans made by government units and nonprofit institutions, even if you were only a co-signer on the loan; domestic support obligations (including spousal and child support, alimony, property settlement debts, attorney fees, and court costs); debts that are the result of willful and malicious injury to another party or property of another party; debts for death or personal injury caused by motor vehicle because the debtor was intoxicated by alcohol or drugs; and debts incurred within sixty days of filing a bankruptcy case.

A Complaint to Object to Discharge will be filed by any creditor who believes a debt should not be discharged through bankruptcy. The bankruptcy court will rule on the Complaint once it is filed. Your attorney will charge additional fees to defend against the Complaint, negotiate the matter with the party that filed the Complaint, and appear in court with you.

NOTICE OF CASE FILING When your attorney has prepared the initial bankruptcy documents for your review and signature, all revisions you discuss will be made before filing the case. Once the case has been revised, it is filed by the attorney via computer with the bankruptcy court. **Almost all cases are now filed online, which has dramatically reduced the amount of time it takes to file a bankruptcy.**

When your case is filed, ask your attorney for a copy of the Notice of Case Filing. **Keep this official notice from the court with your important records for a period of seven to ten years.** You may need to refer to this information at some time in the future.

The case number, date of filing, pertinent district/division of the bankruptcy court, and all relevant personal information—such as your address and date of birth—are contained in this document. Only the last four numbers of your social security number should ever be printed on this document or any other documents filed with the court. Your social security number is secure and cannot be viewed by the public.

<u>NOTIFYING CREDITORS</u> You are probably wondering who sends notice of your bankruptcy to creditors. **Creditors receive official notice of your case from the bankruptcy court once the date of the Meeting of Creditors is scheduled.** Realistically this could take two to three weeks once your case is filed, depending on your particular district.

Make sure that your attorney immediately sends individual notices to any creditors that have sued you by mail, fax or email. Until the creditor or their attorney, and the Clerk of Court where the lawsuit was filed receive official notice of your case from your attorney, court proceedings will still take place. If your utilities are at risk of being shut off, your attorney must immediately send notice of your bankruptcy filing to the utility companies to prevent shut-off actions.

This is not necessary in every bankruptcy case that an attorney handles. There will normally be an additional charge to notify each creditor individually. Ask what that fee is before directing your attorney to personally notify any creditors.

O

OPEN COMMUNICATION There will be many legal terms that you don't understand at first. That is to be expected since there is so much that you are hearing for the first time. I have set these terms and the names of documents apart by capitalizing them because they are very important.

If there is little or no communication between you, your attorney, and his or her staff, you are almost guaranteed to be upset with your legal representation. You might even suffer a less-than-desired outcome when your case is over. You must always remember that your attorney works for you. The attorney must continue to answer your questions until you are confident you understand the answers.

If you don't feel your questions are being answered, it might be time to confront the attorney so that you don't have to think about moving on to a different attorney. It is very stressful to change attorneys in the middle of a bankruptcy case. Your life and financial future depend on a good outcome from your bankruptcy case.

OUTCOMES I am sure you're wondering at this point what the outcome of filing bankruptcy will mean for you. Each person's financial situation is different, and it would be impossible to tell you what changes will affect your life after filing. I can tell you this: people almost always feel reduced stress in their lives once they know they are working along with an attorney and his or her staff to solve these financial problems. Your fear of the unknown will soon be a faded memory. The steps necessary to complete a bankruptcy case are now your focus.

P

PARALEGAL A paralegal can be compared to a registered nurse in the medical field. Of course the educational requirements are different for each career.

Paralegals and RNs work in unrelated fields, but each can be considered a bridge to knowledge. I explained to debtors that as a paralegal I'm entrusted with the duty of translating legal terminology into terms that are more easily understood by them. I also explained that it was my job to prepare all documents that the attorney requested in any particular case.

IMPORTANT

Paralegals cannot give you legal advice. Paralegals cannot represent you in court.

There are times when a paralegal accompanies an attorney to court, but he or she is there merely as an administrative aide to the attorney.

Keep the following explanation in mind: An attorney will assess from your beginning point where your ending point is expected to be. In other words they give you advice concerning the *A* and *Z* of the alphabet. Paralegals handle the letters between *A* and *Z* and translate the legal jargon into a language you easily understand.

A competent attorney will have an equally-skilled paralegal. Since this is the person you will deal with most often, request to meet the paralegal at your first or second appointment, and definitely prior to hiring the attorney to work for you.

Be sure that you can communicate well with the paralegal and that you are treated with respect. Remember that paralegals may be much more accessible in the office than the attorney since they generally do not go to court. If you leave a detailed question or message with the paralegal, you are likely to receive a faster response.

Paralegals are trained in customer service and client relations. **They know how to present your questions to the attorney so you receive the most direct answers possible.** An individual works hard to become a good paralegal, and it should be his or her desire to make the process as easy for you as possible.

If a paralegal requests information or documents concerning your case, assist them by providing the information as soon as possible. The attorney needs that information to proceed, and when you provide it quickly, it allows the staff to do their best possible work.

<u>PAY STUBS</u> Your attorney will ask you for all pay stubs you received for the entire six-month period prior to filing bankruptcy. **This information is used to complete the Means Test, which is the first step in determining whether you will file a Chapter 7 or Chapter 13 bankruptcy.**

Most employers will not provide this information directly to your attorney, so it is your responsibility to obtain these pay stubs if you do not have them in your possession. Many employers now offer online access to pay stubs. Ask your payroll department if that option is available to you.

You should keep all pay stubs you receive, even after your case is filed. Your attorney and the trustee may request copies when reviewing your case, especially for the Meeting of Creditors. What you keep now will save you time and effort later.

It is a good habit to keep your pay stubs until you have filed your taxes for the previous tax year. It saves time and trouble later if there is a question about your income figures on the W-2 you receive from your employer.

<u>PENSION INCOME</u> Pension income is income received by someone (or his or her survivor) who was enrolled in a pension program with his or her employer. The payments from pension funds begin when a person is no longer an active employee. This income is added to other types of income for the Means Test.

Normally someone receiving payments from a pension account will also receive a quarterly statement showing that income. These statements can be sent out on a yearly, quarterly, or monthly basis. **Whatever time period pertains to your pension income statement, provide your attorney with all statements pertaining to this income for the past six months.** These are important records that you should keep in a safe place along with your social security statements and annual reports.

<u>**PERSONAL PROPERTY**</u> Personal property is the combination of all of your belongings, cash, financial accounts, household goods, and property other than real estate. Even if you still owe money on your car loan, your vehicle is considered part of your personal property and must be listed.

Other kinds of personal property include: bank accounts; clothing; cash; investment accounts; life insurance policies; household goods and furnishings; jewelry; annuities; firearms and sporting equipment; books, collections, and pictures; security deposits; stocks; boats; and office equipment. Your attorney will ask you to provide a detailed list of this property, along with a yard-sale value for each category.

Since neither your attorney nor the court will personally visit your home to see the property, it is important to provide a complete and accurate list. This ensures that your personal property is correctly listed on your bankruptcy paperwork, and that the exemptions that allow you to keep this property are claimed properly.

The trustee examines this section of your bankruptcy paperwork carefully and is trained to spot discrepancies that could raise red flags regarding your honesty. More often than not, you will be permitted to retain your personal property, so don't be tempted to provide false information. If a trustee senses that you are not being truthful in property matters, it will create major problems for your case. It could even jeopardize your ability to obtain a discharge without losing any property.

<u>**PRIOR BANKRUPTCY FILING(S)**</u> **If you filed bankruptcy before, it is very important that you inform the attorney of the details of that prior case at your first appointment.** The date you filed the prior case, which Chapter you filed, and how and when the case ended will determine the options available to you when you file a new case.

Your attorney should check all national filings from an online database to confirm the information you provide. It will benefit you immensely to be up front with the attorney. **Remember that the attorney works *for* you, not against you. It is important that all information you provide is truthful, accurate, and complete.**

PRIORITY DEBTS Priority debts are those debts owed to the government. They can include: past-due taxes, domestic support obligations, wages owed to employees, contributions to employee benefit plans, and claims for death or personal injury to another party. They will be listed on Schedule E of your bankruptcy paperwork. **These debts are generally non-dischargeable.** Your attorney will advise you about your specific situation.

PURCHASE MONEY SECURITY INTEREST This is the interest a party has in property sold to you that secures what you promised to pay them for that property. Very often when you buy furniture on credit, you will grant a purchase-money security interest to the store where you buy the furniture or to a lending institution that handles the transaction for the retailer.

Some people have been affected by this type of security interest because they purchased tools used in their jobs from a direct-sale tool company. If this pertains to you, let your attorney know as soon as possible since your ability to work depends on those tools. The attorney will handle this issue for you, and the continued use of your tools will not be put at risk.

If you do not pay for the furniture or goods you purchased according to the terms of a credit arrangement, the store can take that property from you. When you file bankruptcy, your attorney may address these claims by filing documents and subsequent court dates specific to your situation. You must fully understand the process prior to giving your attorney permission to pursue any of these actions on your behalf. There will be an additional attorney fee to perform the service appropriate for your situation.

It might be necessary to pay all or a portion of these debts so you can keep the property. You must approve all settlements your attorney reaches with any creditors or the court. It is important for you to discuss any settlements in detail with your attorney and to make the decision that is best for you and your family.

Q

QUALIFIED EDUCATION LOAN This is defined by the IRS as a loan to be used only for qualified higher education expenses. It can be used on behalf of the taxpayer, his or her spouse, or any dependent of the taxpayer. It also includes overpayments made to the taxpayer or individual for the purpose of higher education expenses.

These loans are not always from a non-profit or government source. They are not usually dischargeable in your bankruptcy. Only loans from family members, or an entity owned by the debtor, can be discharged according to bankruptcy law.

QUESTIONS The questions you are asked by your attorney and his or her staff seem never-ending. Answering all of them will guarantee you receive the best legal advice possible. For instance, the attorney may call you with a question at ten a.m., and an hour later the paralegal may call you with "just one more question." Don't be alarmed or begin to second-guess their competency. They are performing the job you have paid them to do, and it takes a team effort to accomplish it well.

Since each person in the attorney's office plays a different role when handling your case, each person you interact with requires different information from you. The staff won't know you spoke to the attorney about something related to the information they are now requesting. Do not become short-tempered with the staff. They are doing what they have been trained to do, and your answers to their questions are vital to the process.

As I stated earlier in the book, you should be the one asking questions. You have probably never gone through this process, and so much of what you are experiencing may be foreign to you. **It is important that you completely understand the process and cooperate fully with your attorney and his or her staff.** You owe it to yourself to make informed decisions and be prepared for the expected outcome of your attorney's advice and actions.

R

REAFFIRMATION AGREEMENT This type of agreement will be discussed with you if you have a mortgage or car loan. There are other types of loans that might also be affected, but these two are the most common.

If you agree to sign a Reaffirmation Agreement, you may essentially give up your opportunity to receive a discharge of that particular debt at a later date. **Even if you lose your job, your health, or your marriage after signing the agreement, you are most likely obligated to pay that specific debt back. You will no longer have protection under the Automatic Stay provided by the bankruptcy case.**

Changes in bankruptcy law have made this type of agreement very common. Debtors often have car loans and mortgages. Prior to 2005 if you continued to make timely payments on these secured debts, you were permitted to keep the property without signing an agreement to do so.

Now you have to sign the Reaffirmation Agreement and abide by its terms in order to keep the house or vehicle secured by the loan. **Your rights under the bankruptcy laws could be affected by signing this agreement. Do not sign it until you fully understand what it means for you.**

If you are not represented by an attorney in your bankruptcy case, the judge of the bankruptcy court could schedule a Hearing to determine that the Reaffirmation Agreement is valid and that you understand what you are signing. The court will then decide if an Order will be entered concerning the validity of the agreement.

Even if you have an attorney, the judge may request a hearing on this matter. Sometimes the court does not rule either in favor of or against a Reaffirmation Agreement. This is a very confusing and important issue, especially since your home or auto may be at risk. Ask your attorney what this could mean for you.

REAL ESTATE Real estate is usually referred to as real property in a bankruptcy case. This includes all real estate in which you have an interest. This could be your home or property you own jointly with your spouse or another party (such as your brothers and sisters). It might even be property you own jointly with an elderly parent. You do not have to reside in the property for the court to consider it your real estate. **All real property you own at the time of filing your bankruptcy case—or that you have sold within the past three years—must be listed in your bankruptcy documents.**

The trustee will want to see copies of all settlement paperwork that concerns property you have sold within the past three years. He or she may also want copies of all deeds you were a party to for at least three years prior to filing bankruptcy. This is a highly scrutinized part of a bankruptcy case.

Report all real estate in which you have any interest to prevent you from having to sort out complicated issues later on. Since most county records are now available online, it will only be a matter of time before the trustee discovers discrepancies in your paperwork that concern real estate transactions.

REAL PROPERTY As I stated in the previous section, real property and real estate are interchangeable terms. In addition to the examples mentioned there, you can own rental or income property, commercial property, or vacant land. These are additional examples of real property.

Full disclosure on your part is required by the court. These assets will not remain hidden for long if you wrongly choose not to disclose them. **The office of the trustee has staff members at its disposal who are well-trained to uncover these types of assets.** As always, honesty is the best policy. Your attorney will be able to advise you about the expected treatment of this type of property in your case and all exemptions that apply to that property.

REDEMPTION OF PROPERTY If you have personal property that is solely for household or family use, you may be able to redeem it in your bankruptcy. **In simpler terms, you can pay the creditor the amount you owe (or**

possibly less) at the time of redemption in order to keep the property. Such property might include jewelry and household furniture. If you pay the amount you owe in one lump sum, and this debt would have been considered dischargeable, you may be permitted to redeem the property and keep it, even after your bankruptcy ends.

Sometimes an attorney can negotiate an amount lower than your actual balance by showing the creditor that the value of the property at the time the case was filed was less than the balance owed. This allows you to retain the property, pay less than you owe, and go on with your life. Often the affected property has sentimental value, such as engagement or wedding rings.

REFINANCE Many people refinance their mortgages prior to meeting with an attorney to discuss bankruptcy. The common reasons for refinancing a mortgage include the following: to reduce interest rates, to use the equity in a home and receive the "cash" out of the property, to pay off high interest credit cards, or to adjust the terms of the mortgage.

It is possible to change the terms of your mortgage during the bankruptcy process, but it is generally done through a Modification Agreement. The mortgage company will ask your attorney to sign an authorization so they are permitted to speak with you directly about this process.

The present economic environment, and the reality of a bleak real estate market, looms ahead of us for some time. These conditions might promote the approval of modification requests. When terms are modified in this way, a mortgage company doesn't have the keys handed back to them, and debtors are permitted the opportunity to remain in their homes while recovering from short-term financial difficulties.

The person seeking the modification must prove that he or she receives enough income to pay the new mortgage payment. Sometimes the lender will not discuss the process unless the mortgage is past-due. **The desire to enter into a Modification Agreement should not be a reason to stop paying your mortgage.** Discuss any questions you have about this procedure with your attorney up front, and be sure your attorney reviews all documents before you sign them.

REPOSSESSION This term is used when discussing property, such as a vehicle or furniture, when you have not paid the creditor according to the terms of the contract.

Lenders holding car loans are required to send notices of repossession to debtors prior to seizing the property. Sometimes mail gets lost on its way to the recipient, and the debtor doesn't know a repossession action is pending. **If you know you are at risk for losing a vehicle to repossession, or you think you might be at risk because you are not making your payments on time, meet with an attorney now to discuss your options.**

Repossessions are especially stressful if your vehicle is taken while you are at work or as you sleep through the night. **Agents hired by a lender to repossess property are knowledgeable about actions that could be taken by debtors to hide the property.** They might even question neighbors about a debtor's daily habits so they can determine the best time to recover the property. **Repossession agents cannot negotiate payment options or extensions of time to pay any past-due amounts when they repossess property.**

If your property is at risk of repossession, contact an attorney today. You don't want to experience the humiliation and expense of discovering the car you drove to work has disappeared. Confront this situation head on, and seek reliable legal advice. Filing bankruptcy could be the best option to prevent repossession.

An important thing to remember is that the attorney will need time to properly prepare a bankruptcy case for filing. **The sooner you discuss the possibility of repossession with an attorney, the sooner the stress of the situation will be defused. You will be able to go to work without worrying about losing your car.**

Once your bankruptcy case is filed, a creditor has to request permission from the bankruptcy court to regain control of any property. The creditor or their attorney will file an action called a Motion for Relief from Automatic Stay for this purpose. The Automatic Stay that goes into effect when you file protects your property until the court rules on any Motion for Relief from Stay actions filed by a creditor. **If relief from the Automatic Stay is granted by the court, the creditor is allowed to retrieve the property even though you have a bankruptcy case in place.**

<u>RESPONSIBILITY</u> Each party to a contract or agreement has to uphold certain responsibilities. As the debtor you have the responsibility to repay

the debt you owe according to the contract. A creditor must also fulfill their responsibilities as outlined in the agreement.

Once either party defaults on contractual duties, the ability to maintain a good working relationship deteriorates. Many people are pushed toward filing bankruptcy because interest rates skyrocket on their credit cards. One person used her credit cards to finance fertility treatments with the intent to repay the balances. Sadly the credit card companies nearly tripled the interest rate on those balances, and she was unable to pay even the minimum payments each month. Sadder yet she was not able to conceive, and she was haunted by the disappointment every day since she still owed such an exorbitant amount on the cards.

Sometimes the debtor in a bankruptcy case is owed money by another person. Perhaps a family member or close friend promised to pay him or her back. But guess what—he or she didn't pay the money back, and the person who loaned the money had no choice but to file bankruptcy to get out from under the debt.

There are many responsibilities that are not upheld in the financial world. **Thankfully those who qualify to file bankruptcy can pursue a fresh start, and then take the necessary steps toward becoming more responsible about their finances.**

I worked with debtors who hid their gambling debts from loved ones, only to find themselves buried under that debt. Shopping and gambling beyond what your extra income allows is more common that you think. **Don't run away from the responsibility to get help if you need it, and correct any habits now that could lead you into trouble again.**

S

SCHEDULES The Schedules in a bankruptcy case refer to individual sections of your paperwork. Each Schedule lists specific information in detail, including income, property, creditors, and exemptions. **You will review and approve these Schedules along with the attorney when you sign your bankruptcy paperwork. It might be necessary to file amendments to these Schedules after your case is filed.** It is part of the bankruptcy process.

The explanations provided by the bankruptcy court for each Schedule are included below, along with some minor clarifications. Schedules A through J consist of the following:

Schedule A: Real Property

(A list of all real estate in which you or your spouse have any legal or future interest, including community property, life estate, and co-ownership)

Schedule B: Personal Property

(A list of personal property of all kinds of the debtor and spouse, including: the type of property; owned by husband, wife, or jointly; description and location of the property; current value of debtor's interest in the property before deducting any loans on the property)

Schedule C: Exemptions

(A list of all exempt property from Schedules A and B, including: the law allowing the exemption, the value of the exemption, and the current value of the property before deducting the exemption)

Schedule D: Secured Creditors

(A list of all creditors who can take property back if you don't continue to pay them, including: the creditor's name, bankruptcy notices address, account number, which party owes the debt [either husband, wife, or joint], date of claim [when the loan began], nature of the debt [mortgage, vehicle loan, etc.], the amount of the claim [balance], any unsecured portion of the loan [the difference between what the property is worth and what you owe on it])

Schedule E: Unsecured Priority Creditors

(A list of domestic support obligation arrearages; wages owed to employees; contributions to employee benefit plans; claims of certain farmers and fishermen; security deposits for purchase or lease of property; taxes and debts owed to the government; claims on commitments to FDIC, etc.; claims for death or personal injury to another while intoxicated)

Schedule F: Unsecured Creditors

(A list of credit cards, medical bills, personal loans, etc., including: the name and bankruptcy address of creditors; whether or not there is a co-debtor; who owes debt: husband, wife, or joint; date the account opened and for what purpose, such as: credit card, personal loan, medical bill, etc.; amount of claim [balance])

Schedule G: Executory Contracts and Unexpired Leases

(A list of all executory contracts or leases of real or personal property, including timeshares)

Schedule H: Co-Debtors

(A list of any and all co-debtors for each account with a co-debtor, including name and address)

Schedule I: Current Income of Individual Debtor(s)

(A list of all income received by debtor and spouse, including: gross income, detailed payroll deductions, income from operation of business, rental income, alimony, support, pension or retirement income, social security income, any other income not already listed)

Schedule J: Current Expenditures of Individual Debtor(s)

(A list of all expenses, including: rent or mortgage; property insurance; real estate taxes; utilities, such as electricity, heating fuel, telephone, cable, etc.;

home maintenance; food; clothing purchased on a monthly basis; medical and dental expenses not covered by insurance; transportation, including: gas, oil, tires, etc.; charitable contributions; insurance premiums not listed on your pay stubs; alimony or support you pay; expenses for any dependents not living with you; and business expenses. Your attorney will ask for a detailed list of these expenses. Compile this list before you meet with the attorney so you receive the best advice possible.)

SECURED CREDITORS These creditors retain a security interest in and ownership of property until you pay your obligation to them in full. **Some examples of secured creditors are mortgage companies, banks that provide car loans, and lenders that grant home equity loans.**

The most important thing to remember about secured creditors is that they will use all means necessary to retrieve the property that secures the loan if you do not pay according to the terms of your contract. **Once you make a late payment, you default on the contract. That delinquency could set a chain of collection efforts in motion.**

If you ever signed mortgage documents, you know just how many pages of legalese they contain. Printed somewhere in the midst of that stack of paper are the terms that outline how and when the lender can take the property back from you if you do not pay on time.

It is difficult to negotiate with a creditor if you are past-due on your loan or if you are avoiding calls from the creditor. **Stay in touch with a creditor when you find yourself in a financial bind, and try to keep the lines of communication open.**

SECURITY INTEREST The bank or mortgage company that loaned you money to purchase a home or car holds a security interest in that property until you pay it off in full.

A creditor's security interest is equal to the balance on your loan. You may disagree with that assumption and believe that the property is now worth substantially less than what you owe. In this case your attorney may suggest filing a Motion to Value Secured Property with the court. This is a common practice to attempt to decrease the claim that a secured creditor receives in a Chapter 13 bankruptcy case.

Your attorney will charge an additional fee to file this Motion, but it could benefit you if the Motion is granted. Ask your attorney to explain this area of the law in detail and how filing a motion of this type might work to your advantage.

SOCIAL SECURITY INCOME Income received as social security or social security-disability benefits will not be counted toward your Means Test. Disability checks received by veterans may also be excluded.

This might be the only income you receive. Not having to include this income in your Means Test might allow you to qualify to file a Chapter 7 bankruptcy instead of Chapter 13.

These types of income are listed on Schedule I in the appropriate column even if they are not included in the Means Test. **Give your attorney a copy of the most recent annual statement from the federal government showing the total you receive each month from social security or social security/ disability.** This statement shows the amount of gross income you receive and the amount that is deducted for health insurance. The insurance premium will be listed as a monthly expense on your Schedule J.

STATEMENT OF FINANCIAL AFFAIRS This portion of the paperwork gives the trustee a snapshot view of your financial transactions for the past two to three years. You must provide the following information to your attorney so this section can be properly completed:

Section 1: Income from employment or operation of business

Latest paystubs from all sources, W-2's for last two years, gross income from operation of a business year-to-date, and total for each of last two years for operation of a business

Section 2: Income other than from employment or operation of business

Statements of social security or disability income year-to-date and for each of the last two years; amounts received in alimony or child support; income from any other sources such as pension, IRAs, stock sales, or annuities

Section 3: Payments to creditors

Detailed information about all payments you made to creditors within the last ninety days that were more than $600, payments made to family members or businesses you are a part of to repay loans within the last year

Section 4: Suits and administrative proceedings, executions, garnishments, and attachments

Information on all lawsuits you are a part of within the past year. This includes civil actions filed against you, such as: divorce, mortgage foreclosure actions, and also lawsuits you have filed. Any property that was seized within the past year and the information regarding the party that seized it must also be provided.

Section 5: Repossessions, foreclosures, and returns

A list of all repossessions within the past year, including: the name of the creditor, the date the repossession took place, the type of property repossessed, and the value of that property at the time. The party that took the property back should have provided you with a detailed statement of those amounts after the repossession.

Section 6: Assignments and receiverships

Any property that was assigned for the benefit of a creditor within the last 120 days, or any property that is in the hands of a court-appointed official within the past year. This generally pertains to people who own businesses.

Section 7: Gifts

List any gifts or charitable donations within the last year that exceed $200 per family member or more than $100 per charity here. This includes donations made to a religious organization for any purpose, including weekly offerings, tithes, or donations

Section 8: Losses

A list of any losses you have experienced in the last year, including: stolen property, property damage from fire or storms. Provide documentation from the insurance company that shows you received less than the property value, including any deductibles you paid.

Section 9: Payments related to debt counseling or bankruptcy

A list of payments related to debt counseling or bankruptcy. You may have signed up for debt counseling or consolidation and the fees you paid should be entered in this section. Provide the name, address, date, and amount you paid for these services in the past year, including fees paid to attorneys regarding bankruptcy.

Section 10: Other transfers

List of all property you transferred to another party within the past two years. Include copies of stock sales, settlement sheets from the sale of real estate, and withdrawals from IRAs. Written statements must be provided to your attorney because the trustee will ask to see them prior to or at your Meeting of Creditors.

Section 11: Closed financial accounts

A list of all financial accounts you have closed within the past year. This includes bank accounts, retirement accounts, and pension funds. If your bank closed your account for any reason, you should also include that information here. The name, address, account number, balance at the time the account was closed, and type of account must be provided.

Section 12: Safe deposit boxes

Provide the name and address of the bank where you have your safe deposit box. Also list what is held in that box, such as: important papers, jewelry, passports, etc.

Section 13: Setoffs

List all actions taken by your bank within the past ninety days to remove funds from your account without your permission and then use them to pay a past-due account you have with that bank.

Section 14: Property held for another person

List all property you control that is owned by another person. These include: accounts where you are a signer on an elderly parent's checking account, accounts where you act as a trustee or guardian for someone else, and educational funds set up for your children or grandchildren, etc.

Section 15: Prior address of debtor

List your prior address if you have not been at your current address for at least three years. Provide all addresses necessary to cover a three-year period. Include the names you used and the time period you resided at each address.

Section 16: Spouses and former spouses

List all former spouses within the past eight years, either from divorce or death; list the name of your current spouse if he or she is not filing bankruptcy with you, even if you are separated.

Section 17: Environmental information

List any environmental law violations you have been involved in, including: site name, governmental unit name and address, docket number and status of violation. This pertains to local, state, and federal regulations.

Section 18: Nature, location, and name of business

(This section pertains to anyone involved in a business for any part of the past six years. If this is the case for you, continue reading Sections nineteen through twenty-five. Otherwise, skip to the next topic below.)

List the nature, name, and location of any and all businesses you are or have been involved in for the past eight years.

Section 19: Books, records, and financial statements

List the bookkeepers and accountants involved in each business for the past two years. Also provide all firms who have audited the books of the business within two years, and those to whom you have provided financial statements within that time period.

Section 20: Inventories

List the dates of the last two inventories taken on your business property and include the information concerning the person who conducted or supervised the inventory.

Section 21: Current partners, officers, directors, and shareholders

List all current partners, officers, directors, and shareholders with an interest in any partnership you are involved in.

Section 22: Former partners, officers, directors, and shareholders

List all former partners within the past year and the date they withdrew from the partnership.

Section 23: Withdrawals from a partnership or distributions by a corporation

List all withdrawals or distributions credited to or given to any insider of the partnership or corporation within the past year.

Section 24: Tax consolidation group

List the name and Federal Tax ID number of any parent corporation within the past six years.

Section 25: Pension funds

Provide the name and Federal Tax ID number of any pension fund that you have been responsible for as an employer within the past six years.

STATEMENT OF INTENTION In a Chapter 7 bankruptcy, this portion of the paperwork lists secured creditors and the property that secures those loans (such as a mortgage or car loan). **The Statement of Intention is a document signed by you that informs the court, and your creditors, about your decision to either keep or give back the property that secures a debt.**

If you wish to retain your home or car, review this document to confirm that it states that you want to reaffirm on these debts. If you want to give up your home or car, it should state that you want to surrender this property.

Creditors involved in your case will be able to view documents on the bankruptcy website and should mark their records accordingly. Your attorney will be contacted by creditors after your case is filed to confirm your intentions on particular debts. If further action is required on your part, your attorney will advise you accordingly.

STUDENT LOANS Loans you have received specifically to pay for higher education either for yourself, your spouse, or your child must be listed in your bankruptcy paperwork. These loans are normally backed by the US government and are not considered dischargeable debts. **Even though you have filed bankruptcy, you will probably have to pay these loans back once the bankruptcy case has ended.** Your attorney can advise you completely in your particular situation.

T

TAX LIENS If you have suffered at the hands of the IRS, you know that dealing with a tax lien can be a devastating financial problem.

Maybe after your tax return was reviewed, it was determined that you owed more taxes than you paid at the time you filed the return. You now owe the additional tax, along with interest and penalties. When will it ever end?

Unfortunately the IRS has quite a backlog of work, so you won't be notified immediately if there are errors on your tax return. You didn't know until the bill came that you had an unpaid tax bill looming over you.

There was no need to put money away toward an unexpected tax bill. Unable to pay the tax in full when the notice came in, you read on the notice that you should call the IRS immediately to make arrangements to pay the amount due. I know—calling the IRS was the last thing you wanted to do.

Time has passed and the IRS filed a lien against your property. That allowed them to freeze your bank account. You can't even access enough money to put gas in the car or food in the refrigerator.

There may be a way out of this mess. If you have received a notice of a pending lien, or if the lien has already been attached to your personal and/or real property, contact an attorney right now. Filing bankruptcy may release the lien from your property and bank accounts. **This is a very serious issue. The lien will stay in place until you have paid the taxes or you have taken** other measures to correct the problem. Filing bankruptcy may be exactly what you need to do if you are facing this serious situation.

TAX RETURNS One major requirement of the bankruptcy law is that your federal income tax returns must be filed with the IRS, up to and including the most recent tax year. You must provide copies of tax returns for the past two years to your attorney. A copy of the most recent return must be filed with the court, and your attorney will send a copy to the appropriate trustee. If you do not have copies of these returns, refer to the next section concerning tax transcripts.

Your case will not be discharged until this obligation is fulfilled. A bankruptcy case can be dismissed if the debtor doesn't provide copies of tax returns or transcripts to the court.

TAX TRANSCRIPTS It is surprising how many people don't save copies of their tax returns. Copies may not be available to you for some other reason. They may have been destroyed in a flood or fire, or a spouse won't provide them to you because of a difficult divorce. If you do not have a copy of your latest return, request a tax transcript from the IRS immediately. A tax transcript provides sufficient information for the bankruptcy trustees. A transcript is not an actual copy of the return you filed, but is instead a summary of all entries made on the tax return.

There is currently no charge for a tax transcript from the IRS. The request does take a bit of time to process, however. Your attorney can assist you in requesting this document from the IRS. The transcript can be provided by the IRS either to you or to your attorney, whichever you prefer. If you ask the IRS to provide the transcript directly to your attorney, request a copy of it from the attorney for your own records. There is a fee to receive actual copies of your federal income tax return from the IRS.

You can obtain a copy of your tax transcript from the IRS website: http://www.irs.gov. Click on "Order a Tax Return or Transcript" and follow the instructions for the appropriate request.

TRUSTEE As I have mentioned many times throughout this book, the bankruptcy court appoints a trustee to oversee every bankruptcy case. The trustee does not represent you or the creditors in your bankruptcy. This official is appointed by the court to ensure that you meet all of the requirements under the federal bankruptcy law and that all parties in the case are treated fairly.

The property you own or that is in your possession at the time your case is filed remains under the control of the bankruptcy court until your case is either discharged or dismissed. You may not sell your car or home, incur new debt, or put property into someone else's name during the bankruptcy process unless you first receive permission from the trustee to do so.

The trustee also determines what property will be exempt from creditors. This simply means that exempt property will not be sold to pay creditors. The office of the US Trustee determines the value of all exemptions according to the type of property involved, such as: real property, clothing, retirement funds, household goods, automobiles, and bank accounts.

Any property that is determined to be worth more than the exemptions allowed for that type of property can be subject to liquidation by the court. Hiring a knowledgeable attorney will provide you with an accurate picture of what will happen to your property in your bankruptcy case.

An experienced attorney will know the exemption values for each category of property that you own. Prospective attorneys must be able to answer your questions completely and intelligently to demonstrate to you that they have the expertise necessary to represent you.

U

UNDUE HARDSHIP The court sometimes encounters a situation that is considered an undue hardship for a debtor. This can relate to repayment of a student loan or another debt when the budget or health of the debtor does not allow it.

You can deal directly with a lender to determine their guidelines when considering the repayment of a loan an undue hardship. These legal terms are found in the fine print of the loan documents you originally signed. It is best to locate these original loan documents before asking your attorney if the loan repayment could be considered an undue hardship by the lender or the court.

Short of the death or permanent disability of the debtor, it is not likely that the court will determine that a loan repayment presents an undue hardship to the debtor. See what your attorney believes the outcome of pursuing a claim of undue hardship could be in your particular situation.

UNITED STATES TRUSTEE The office of the United States Trustee controls the process of filing bankruptcy in the United States. This office determines how bankruptcy law is implemented. **The office of the United States Trustee oversees what each trustee considers a violation of any provision of the law and the property that exceeds the exemptions allowed by law.**

Your property is under the control of the US Trustee once your bankruptcy case is filed. That control continues until your case has concluded, and also for a period of time beyond dismissal or discharge of your case. The US Trustee can direct Chapter 7 and 13 trustees to monitor the assets of individuals who have filed bankruptcy even after their cases have been discharged. The US Trustee can also delay the discharge of a case until any lawsuits involving personal injury and/or the administration of an estate have been completed.

The office of the US Trustee represents the interests of the US government in all bankruptcy matters. You may never meet face-to-face with the US Trustee or anyone from his or her office, but these individuals are actively involved in each bankruptcy case that is filed.

UNSECURED CREDITORS Unsecured creditors are the most common creditors in bankruptcy cases. Unsecured debts can include credit card bills, unsecured loans, medical bills, utility bills, magazine subscriptions, student loans, deficiency balances from repossessions, dental bills, veterinarian bills, heating oil bills, and any other creditors that do not hold security until a debt is repaid.

If you are unable to pay any of these bills when they are due, it is a sign that you may have reached the point where you are insolvent. Find out if filing bankruptcy is practical in your situation.

Explore how the law pertains to you and how your bankruptcy filing will affect your current financial situation. After hiring the right attorney, a Means Test will be performed to see what Chapter of the Bankruptcy Code will be the best for you to file.

Obtain sound legal advice and take the appropriate steps in the right direction. Your financial future will look brighter than it has in the past.

V

VALUATION OF PROPERTY Depending on the type of property you own or have in your possession, the attorney or the court may ask you to obtain a valuation of that property. If you own real estate, the court needs to know the fair market value of the real estate as of the date you file bankruptcy. If you own precious jewelry or gun collections, expect the court to ask you to have them appraised by a certified appraiser.

You should print out a copy of the current market value of all vehicles in your name at the time of filing. Some of the websites you can use to do this are listed below:

http://www.kbb.com
http://www.cars.com
http://www.edmunds.com
http://www.nadaguides.com

The preceding suggestions do not suggest a preference for or reliance upon any of these sources for the actual values of vehicles in your legal matters. Your attorney has the final word on what source or sources you should use.

Since you readily know the details about your vehicles, such as the specific options on your car and the actual mileage, you should obtain these values yourself and then provide a printout of the value of each vehicle to your attorney. **The bankruptcy court usually takes into account the private** party value of each of your vehicles. Be accurate when obtaining these values and you will avoid complications from the trustee later.

VALUES There are many factors that affect a person's view of bankruptcy and his or her decision to file or not to file a bankruptcy case. These factors are based on individual and family values, religious teachings, work ethic, fears of what others will think, and ideas about personal responsibility.

Take comfort in knowing that filing bankruptcy is not a crime. In actuality it is perfectly legal and is utilized by thousands of respectable people each and every year. Filing a bankruptcy case is not a reflection on your personal beliefs or character. Bankruptcy is simply a legal, financial tool that allows you to react appropriately to situations, often beyond your control, that involve debt and finances.

Money problems can be created by major fluctuations in your budget. Some of the causes of these fluctuations include losing your job, suffering a sudden illness, or increases in interest rates on your debts. Most of these situations are inevitable. Your level of preparedness when devastation unexpectedly hits will greatly influence your ability to ride out a financial storm.

Delaying your decision to meet with an attorney, or putting off filing bankruptcy when you are advised it is the best option, could unnecessarily deplete funds that you have put away for your retirement or that you expect to use for other purposes.

Do not allow your fears of the unknown, or any personal feelings of guilt or shame, to slam the door on bankruptcy. Society has moved beyond the beliefs of past generations who imposed a sense of shame on someone who found it necessary to file bankruptcy. We face very different times when it comes to the economy and our involvement in it. The bottom has literally fallen out of our job security and financial freedom.

Get past the guilt and feelings of shame as soon as you can. Others don't believe you should feel guilty or shameful in your situation.

Your physical and emotional health is much more important than maintaining your credit rating or paying back every penny of your debts. Now is the time to value yourself and look forward to your future.

Some debtors find it beneficial to donate their time and energy to a charity or volunteer group while they go through bankruptcy. It gives them a sense of well-being and self-respect. You may consider this if you have a hard time accepting the situation or the steps necessary to move beyond your current dilemma. Many people will benefit from your efforts.

VOLUNTARY DISMISSAL Since you file bankruptcy voluntarily, it is also possible to dismiss your bankruptcy voluntarily. No one has forced you to enter into a bankruptcy case, and you will not be forced to remain in that case. In certain instances, people benefit from some type of financial windfall that allows them to dismiss their case and pay off their creditors. These might include a settlement or award from a personal injury case, the receipt of life insurance proceeds or beneficiary funds in an estate, or receipt of a severance or retirement package.

When you dismiss your bankruptcy case voluntarily or when the court orders the dismissal of the case, you no longer have protection under the bankruptcy laws. **Creditors can take legal actions against you to recover the debts you owe them. Repossessions and mortgage foreclosure actions will be allowed to proceed once a case is dismissed.**

Your decision to direct the court to dismiss your bankruptcy case is an important one. It should only be made after receiving legal advice from your attorney. **The circumstances surrounding your desire to dismiss the case are critical to the advice you will receive from the attorney. Inform your attorney accurately and completely about those details if you are contemplating dismissal of your case.**

W

WHAT DO YOU DO NOW? Without a doubt, continue to learn about the bankruptcy process, and take the advice of the attorney involved in your case along the way. You will improve your state of mind by doing these things, knowing that you are taking important steps toward a brighter future.

Relieving the stress in your life just one step at a time will allow you to breathe easier, feel better, and wake up each morning with a more positive outlook. Keep taking one informed step at a time. Your journey will lead you to a better place.

WORKERS' COMPENSATION If you have been injured at work, you know what it means to collect Workers' Compensation. Your checks are much smaller than they were before you were injured on the job. Sadly your bills have not reduced in size. Your expenses have probably risen because traveling to and from medical appointments increase the cost of filling up your tank. Taking on overtime hours or a second job are no longer options you can take advantage of in order to improve your financial position.

Workers' Compensation income will be counted toward gross income on the Means Test to determine which Chapter of bankruptcy you will file. Provide written copies of your Workers' Compensation Benefit Statement to the attorney.

X

X-CEL AT REALISTIC SPENDING Make conscientious financial choices and think before you reach into your wallet to make frivolous purchases. People tend to reward themselves for doing good deeds. They also attempt to heal their wounds by buying something special. I know. In my first year of widowhood I could be found in the jewelry store on a regular basis.

Find healthy ways to work through stress and realistic ways to reward yourself. Curb spending on unnecessary items and you will have more money to splurge on something truly worthwhile in the long run. Become the bargain shopper in your circle of friends, and you'll find that you receive more compliments than someone who overpays for items on a regular basis.

You could learn to cook. I know it sounds corny, but it is always cheaper to make meals at home. Express yourself through cooking and make a challenging new recipe every week. It will make your life more interesting and you'll develop culinary skills at the same time.

When you do go out to treat yourself, don't let people pressure you into spending more than you planned. They have their budget, you have yours. Set ground rules before you go out with others and there won't be any surprises when it comes time to pay the check.

Make wise choices about the money you spend.

Y

YOU CAN CHANGE YOUR LIFE Think of this situation as one of the most important financial challenges you have faced in your life. **You've learned things from this challenge no other life lesson could have taught you.**

Make good choices concerning your finances from now on. Feeling bogged down in a quagmire of debt and indecision negatively affected your life. You chose to move beyond the distress. **Live by the budget you've created, and find ways to correct those bad habits that cause you to spend more than you earn.**

Many people learn to live within their means after completing bankruptcy. **Only purchase what you can truly afford, and save toward those things you desire down the road.** You will regain and maintain control of your money and contentment. Practice what you've learned about managing your income and expenses. You will enjoy a bright future and be a positive influence on everyone who comes into contact with you.

Z

ZEST FOR LIFE Now that you've reached the end of the book you've learned many things about your finances and bankruptcy. You know that following a budget will keep you focused, and the legal terminology that fills your head finally makes sense.

You realize your zest for life is a treasured thing, and worrying about financial problems has stolen some joy from you. Financial problems diminished your energy and prevented you from looking toward the future. If you have chosen to file bankruptcy, the negativity and stress will soon be things of the past.

I know you have the ability to recapture the fun-loving, light-hearted way of life. Imagine yourself in a convertible on a beautiful sunny day. The wind is blowing, and you've tuned the radio to your favorite station. There is nothing ahead of you but open road. **You have choices to make when you come to the exit ramps of life, and making the right choices will now be easier. You just needed a little encouragement and common-sense information to guide you.**

Get out there and enjoy life again. Find an activity that makes you happy and make sure you fit it into your schedule. **Use the tools you've discovered to live a good life, but always remember to prepare for that rainy day.** It will inevitably rain in your life. Unexpected things happen, and life takes twists and turns. That much is certain. Prepare for the inevitable storm and it will pass by quickly.

Conclusion

You arrived at a place and time in your life that was both unexpected and life-changing. That is what prompted you to obtain this book.

The desire for a better future is what gave you the strength to read it as your roadmap out of the financial wilderness. **I want you to know I'm proud of you for working toward leaving this crisis behind you once and for all.**

Only you know the personal reasons behind this financial crisis in your life. You may have lost your job, faced a health problem, or found it too easy to spend more than you could repay. Maybe you were involved in a divorce or suffered the death of a loved one or spouse. The reasons could be any of these, a combination of them, or countless others.

You have now learned that guilt is not beneficial, and what other people think about you and your decisions does not matter.

From now on you can expect to move beyond this crisis to a better, more positive and prosperous life. It is entirely possible, and I am confident that you will make the most of your financial future.

You educated yourself by reading this book and hiring a qualified attorney to work with you toward a common goal. **It is now only a matter of time before your life begins to improve dramatically.**

Congratulations! You took that first superhero step and you are now ready to complete your journey. I assure you, the first step was the hardest of all. Facing your fears and taking unknown trails is always difficult. Each new step will bring challenges and opportunities into your life. What you learned from this book and your attorney will equip you to make the most of each day. Use this guide to move beyond your current situation toward:

FINANCIAL HOPE AND FREEDOM

www.ingramcontent.com/pod-product-compliance
Lightning Source LLC
Chambersburg PA
CBHW060558200326
41521CB00007B/605